THE JAPANESE SWORD

VICTORIA & ALBERT MUSEUM • FAR EASTERN SERIES

THE JAPANESE SWORD
THE SOUL OF THE SAMURAI

GREGORY IRVINE

WEATHERHILL

First edition, 2000

© 2000 The Board of Trustees of the
Victoria and Albert Museum

Published by Weatherhill, Inc., 41 Monroe Turnpike,
Trumbull CT O 6611, by special arrangement with the
Victoria and Albert Museum.

Gregory Irvine asserts his moral right
to be identified as the author of this book.

ISBN 0-8348-0475-1

Designed by Harry Green

Printed in Hong Kong

Every effort has been made to seek permission to
reproduce those images whose copyright does not
reside with the V&A, and we are grateful to the
individuals and institutions that have assisted in this
task. Any omissions are entirely unintentional and
details should be addressed to the publishers.

Illustrations

JACKET FRONT Detail from plate 15.

JACKET BACK (LEFT) plate 30.

JACKET BACK (RIGHT) Detail from plate 7.

HALF TITLE Woodblock print (*c*.1850) by Ichikawa
Yoshikazu entitled 'Kyoto Shijō Nawate Gassen'
(Battle of Shijō Nawate at Kyoto). This gory battle
scene of the wars of the Nambokuchō period depicts
the hero Kusunoki Masasure fighting against the
army of Ashikaga Takauji and was the type of popular
print which stimulated national pride in the legacy
of the samurai. V&A: E.13696–1886.

FRONTISPIECE 'Ehon Musashi Abumi' (Picture Book of
the Stirrups of Musashi) by Katsushika Hokusai, 1836.
'Lord Soga no Iruka, the Enemy of the State' is depicted
fighting his assassins during the coup d'état of AD 645
known as the *Taika no Kaishin*.
V&A: E.15071–1886

PAGE 5 Plate 9, left.

Japanese Historical Periods

Yayoi	*c*.300 BC–*c*.AD 300
Kofun	*c*.300–710
Nara	710–794
Heian	794–1185
Kamakura	1185–1333
Muromachi	1333–1568
(Nambokuchō	1337–1392)
(Sengoku	1467–1568)
Azuchi-Momoyama	1568–1600
Edo	1600–1868
Meiji	1868–1912
Taishō	1912–1926
Shōwa	1926–1989
Heisei	1989–

Contents

Acknowledgements

My thanks are due to many people for the assistance and encouragement provided both during the writing of this book and the many years leading up to it. Primarily to Victor Harris, Keeper of Japanese Antiquities at the British Museum, with whom I have had the pleasure of working in my early museum career and with whom I have also spent many fruitful hours both in the UK and Japan. To Nobuo Ogasawara and Hiroshi Ikeda of the Tokyo National Museum; Tomoyasu Kubo of the Kyoto National Museum; Toyozo Sato of the Tokugawa Museum, Nagoya; Yoshihiko Fukui at Atsuta Jingu, Nagoya, and Takaya Miyamoto of the Hayashibara Corporation, Okayama, all of whom have given freely of their time and knowledge during my visits to Japan. Also to my longtime friends Toyoko and Hiroshi Kondo, who have provided support, encouragement (and accommodation) during my many research periods in Japan, and to Yumiko Yamamori, who has over the years provided invaluable help with the reading of difficult Japanese inscriptions. To the Bunkachō, the Japanese Agency for Cultural Affairs, who funded a considerable research period in Japan. To the Daiwa Foundation and the Sasakawa Foundation, two UK-based Japanese charitable organizations who have also funded research periods in Japan. To Ian Thomas of the V&A's Photographic Department for his patience and skills in photographing the extremely demanding Japanese swords in our collection. To the V&A itself, which has provided the essential funding to extend my research periods in Japan as well as giving me the time and opportunity to produce this book in the Research Department. This, perhaps unique institution within museums provides a form of in-house sabbatical during which an individual is given exclusive time to concentrate on a particular project.

Finally my thanks are due to my family, Harriet, Dan and Grace, who have endured my many extended absences in Japan and who I hope will one day accompany me to Japan itself and see for themselves the source of so much disruption in their lives!

Detail of the centre panel
of the Battle of Shijō Nawate
shown on half-title page

Introduction

The Japanese sword has a unique place among the world's weaponry. Perhaps in no other society has technology produced such a superb cutting weapon which is held in high esteem due to both its effectiveness in battle and the spiritual qualities it is believed to contain. Its efficiency is such that it can cut through armour without breaking or bending, and its spirituality is marked by the religious rites involved in its production.

The Japanese sword as we know it today was perfected nearly 1,000 years ago and evolved from prototypes introduced into Japan from mainland Asia around the beginning of the Christian Era. The sword in many cultures has long been recognized as a symbol of power and authority, and in Japan the sword is one of the three items of the imperial regalia, the others being the jewel and the mirror. Legend has it that the imperial sword was taken from the tail of an eight-headed dragon by Susano-ō no Mikoto, the Storm Deity and brother to Amaterasu Ōmikami, the Sun Goddess from whom the imperial lineage claimed descendance. Many other myths have evolved around the sword and those who have used it. In the popular imagination, both in Japan and the West, the samurai of Japan's long and turbulent years of civil war who travels the country dispensing sudden and violent justice, yet retaining his honour, is not dissimilar to the Western myth of the gun-carrying hero of the American West who equally dispensed justice in a lawless society.

The sword was the indispensable weapon of the samurai and a symbol of his authority which had stood for generations, thereby forming a continuity of military and spiritual power and representing his attitude to life itself. He should be prepared to combine his physical strength with his inner spirit and have the inner resolution to use the sword at a moment's notice to kill, or be killed in the service of his master. The importance and significance of the sword to the warrior are perhaps best summed up in the traditional Japanese saying: 'The sword is the soul of the samurai.' The Japanese word used for soul, *kokoro*, contains the meaning of both spirit and heart.

Japanese swords have, from early times, been dedicated to Shintō shrines where the blades themselves are often regarded as a physical manifestation of the *kami*, the numinous spirits or natural powers which are revered or venerated in the Shintō belief. Swords also have strong connections with Buddhism, and the Buddhist guardian deities, the Niō, who stand at the entrance to many temples, can be seen holding swords. The Buddhist deity Fudō Myō-Ō (who often appears carved into a sword blade) also bears a sword to suppress evil. The preservation of swords in shrines and temples, together with the tradition of signing and dating blades on the tang means that the changes and development of the Japanese sword can be followed with some accuracy for a considerable historical period. It is also possible to see how changes in forms of warfare in Japan, which continued in one form or another until the early seventeenth century, are reflected in the shape of the sword itself.

The beauty of the Japanese sword lies in the steel of the blade, rather than in the purely functional aspects of an efficient weapon designed to kill. The traditional methods of forging the blade involve the combination of different grade billets of steel which are repeatedly folded and hammered together to produce a strong, resilient structure. The ensuing tempering and polishing process produces a finished sword with a hard, razor-sharp edge, backed with a main body of steel which is of a relatively flexible nature. This combination not only results in one of the most practical cutting weapons ever produced, but the processes involved in its manufacture, together with the final polishing, produce a visible grain together with a fine and distinctive crystalline structure all of which are indicative of the date, place and maker of the blade.

Written from a purely Western viewpoint, this book carries with it many of our own perceptions of Japan, and it is hard not to see the sword, an anachronistic weapon in the modern age, as an icon or symbol of Japan itself. This image colours what the Western perception of Japan has long been – a modernized (for this read Westernized) country which still seems to cling to an historical past, real or fabricated. Yet this image of a modern culture which co-exists comfortably with the past is one which the Japanese have themselves perpetuated, and much of the imagery we receive in the West which surrounds the sword and the samurai has been generated in Japan. In the early part of this century when Japan had rapidly become a world power with an army which had contributed to the defeat of the Chinese and a navy which defeated Russia, we in the West were exhibiting in our museums traditional Japanese swords and armour as a visual representation which perpetuated the samurai ethos even in relation to contemporary Japan at that time.

Most Japanese today, especially the young, pay little attention to the historical samurai – except in the ever-popular samurai 'soap-operas' on television. But, to quote a young Japanese acquaintance:

> their [the samurai] mentality of perseverance, loyalty and endeavour to practice Budō [bushidō] is highly appreciated among us even now; especially for the salaried man over forty or so it is a good/useful guide to survive a competitive company life. Among the popular books in Japan today are works with titles such as *To Learn from Oda Nobunaga* and so on.

The translation into English of the seventeenth-century work on strategy, *A Book of Five Rings*, by the samurai Miyamoto Musashi was at one time recommended reading for British businessmen trying to compete with the Japanese.

The very words 'samurai sword' conjure up a string of emotions which are hard to suppress. At the time of writing the British newspapers have been filled with details of an attack in a church where a man went on the rampage with a 'samurai sword'. The use of any other type of sword in such a horrendous attack would not have fired the public imagination in such a way. We are simultaneously repelled and attracted by the romance and the danger associated with this unique weapon.

This book will look at the development of the Japanese sword in an historical context as well as dealing with the emergence of the military class, the samurai, who were the

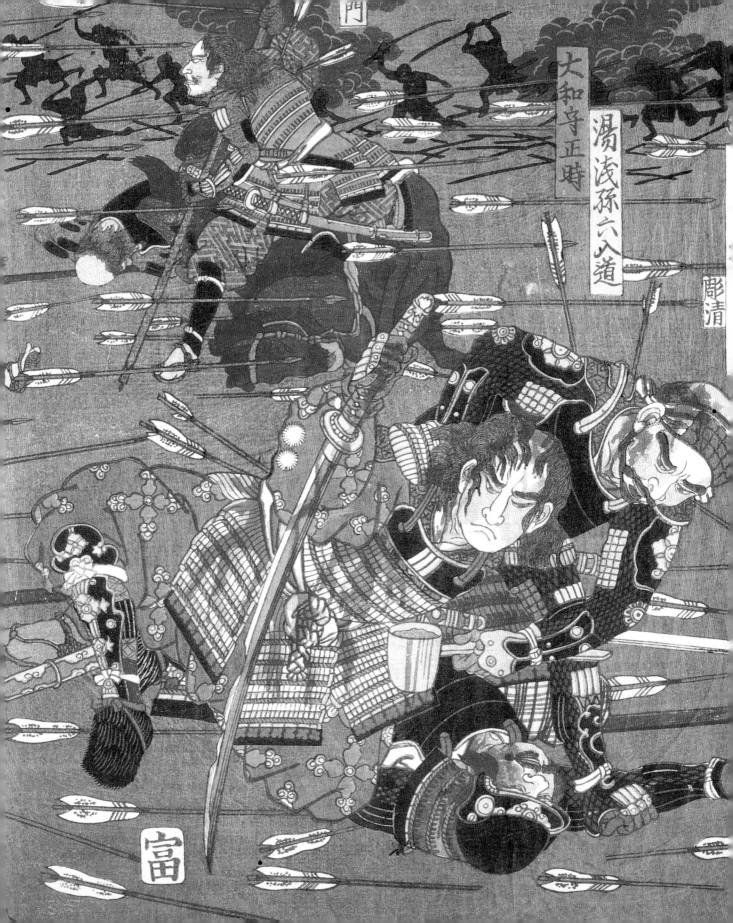

main users of this outstanding weapon. In addition, other weapons associated with the samurai will be discussed; the bow, spears and the gun will also be considered. While drawing wherever possible on swords and weapons within the V&A's own collections, it has been necessary to include material from other collections, particularly from Japan which has, obviously, the best and most well-documented collections of Japanese swords in existence.

The nomenclature used to describe the many features of the Japanese sword is large, varied and at times florid to the point of exasperation. It is, however, precise; and attempts to use English equivalents are often clumsy and can be inaccurate or misleading. There are many books and articles which can help with the understanding and appreciation of the technical aspects of the blade, and this book will not attempt to repeat that which is dealt with by others in greater detail elsewhere. A brief glossary together with outline diagrams will hopefully assist the reader in following some of the more obscure references in the text of this book.

Detail of the right-hand panel
of the Battle of Shijō Nawate
shown on half-title page

1 | Origins of the Japanese Sword

The Japanese sword is a terrible and efficient weapon combining a beauty of form with an elegance of function. It has its origins in the swords produced after the importation of iron-working technology from mainland Asia sometime around the fourth to fifth centuries AD. There had been a brief earlier Bronze Age in Japan during which bronze weapons including spears, swords and halberds had been made, mainly for ritual purposes, using technology imported from China and Korea.

There had been relationships between some of the autonomous, pre-unification kingdoms of Japan and the Chinese empire from as early as the first century AD. Chinese records refer to the despatch of emissaries from Japan and record the gifts they received from the Chinese emperors of the period. Significantly, the Chronicle of the Wei Dynasty (*Wei Zhi*) records that the envoy of Queen Himiko of Yamatai 'from the country of Wa' (Japan) received a gold seal, silks, mirrors and swords in AD 239 from the Wei emperor.

Japan at this time was a country of warring states controlled by various clans all vying for supreme power. The clans moved from Kyūshū, one of the country's southernmost islands, to central Japan where they were eventually unified under the Yamato clan, the ancestors of the Japanese imperial family. Establishing themselves near present-day Nara, the Yamato clan exerted its control over rival clans through a system of loyalty based on kinship and on its own military supremacy. They also built many Kofun, 'Great Tombs', from which the period (c. AD 300–600) is named. These tombs contain much military equipment including armour and horse-trappings as well as swords and examples of the other imperial regalia, the mirror and jewel.

The earliest excavated swords from the Kofun period follow the Chinese style in that they are straight, flat sided and of triangular section (*hira-zukuri*) with a single cutting edge and are exceptional in having the ends of the tang beaten out to form a ring-like pommel. These types of swords are known as *kantō tachi*. The term *tachi* refers to a sword which is worn slung with the cutting edge down and was the standard form of carrying the sword for centuries. Some of these early excavated kantō tachi are richly mounted and have separate, gilded ring-pommels.

Blades of this period have been found which bear inscriptions indicating that they were made in China, and there is little evidence that a fully established sword-producing culture was yet functioning in Japan itself. It is apparent that Chinese blades were held in high esteem and an iron blade of hira-zukuri from a fourth-century tomb at Tōdaijiyama has an inscription which dates it to the Zhongping period (AD 184–9). The inscription refers to the forging process involved in the manufacture of the blade, which has a separate pommel of bronze.

With the introduction of Buddhism from mainland Asia in the sixth century, Japan increasingly adopted many further Chinese philosophical and religious systems as well as its technology. Japan was at this time still not fully unified and the heavily armed Yamato state fought primarily against the Ainu, the indigenous native population of northern Japan, eventually defeating them in AD 792 (although northern Japan retained for centuries a frontier-like state of near lawlessness).

The swords produced during the Nara period (AD 646–794) are known as *chokutō* and, while they are still straight and single-edged in the style of the kantō tachi, a new adaptation to the form of the blade had taken place. This was the introduction of a longitudinal ridge (*shinogi*) on one side of the blade near the cutting edge, the other side of the blade remaining flat. This style of blade is referred to as *katakiri-ha zukuri*. The shinogi was a practical introduction in that it strengthened the physical structure of the blade thereby making the sword less likely to break in combat. Most later Japanese blades have the shinogi on both sides of the blade which results in a much stronger and more efficient sword. The point of the blade (*kissaki*) was small and in this form the sword was most probably wielded in combat with a thrusting technique, rather than used for slashing.

Some fifty-five chokutō have been preserved in the Shōsōin, the imperial repository of the Emperor Shōmu, which was built after his death in AD 756 by his widow, the Empress Kōmyō, to contain his personal effects. This unique repository contains many thousands of treasures from the eighth century. Swords from this period of both Chinese and Japanese manufacture are still in existence today, and through careful maintenance and preservation in Buddhist and Shintō institutions over the centuries the structure of the blades is still clearly visible.

1 The blade known as the 'Suiryū Ken' (Water Dragon Sword) is believed to have been owned by the Emperor Shōmu and was subsequently enshrined together with other of his effects in the Shōsōin by his widow in AD 756. It is a fine example of the chokutō, an early Japanese blade, in katakiri-ha style and was made by early exponents of the Yamato school. The blade was remounted during the nineteenth century in hōken (Treasure Sword) style with fittings by Kanō Natsuo on the direct instructions of the Emperor Meiji.

Collection of the Tokyo National Museum, Important Cultural Property.

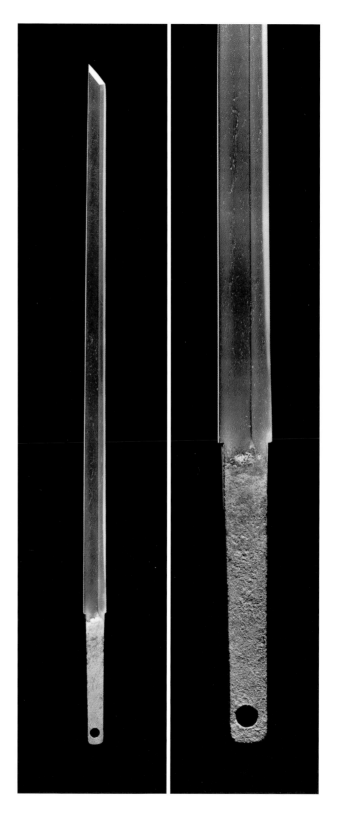

A particular blade which shows the features of the chokutō admirably is the Suiryū Ken, or 'Water Dragon Sword'. This blade was once in the collection of the Shōsōin, but was remounted for the Emperor Meiji in the latter half of the nineteenth century (plate 1). Two blades from the Buddhist temple Shitennōji in Osaka, reputedly belonging to Shotoku Taishi (AD 574–622), the great patron of Buddhism, have in recent years been repolished to show clearly the overall crystalline structure of the blade together with the tempering pattern (*hamon*) near the edge, a feature which is distinctive in all Japanese blades. These types of blades also display an almost imperceptible downward curve known as *uchi-zori* (inner curve). Another feature to develop on blades of the Nara period was the *kissaki moroha*, where the cutting edge extends slightly over the point to the back of the blade.

Blades from the Nara period, many of which were produced in and around Nara itself, were by this time displaying many of the characteristics of all later Japanese blades, whereby a strong, multi-layered structure is produced in a forging process in which different billets of high-grade steel are repeatedly folded and hammered. The resulting tempering, sharpening and polishing of the blade produce a visible crystalline structure wherein lies the beauty of the blade. Such are the recognizable physical characteristics in the structure of the Nara-period swords that the terminology used to describe later blades can equally be used for these early blades.

The making of the Japanese sword

It would be informative at this point to describe the processes involved in the production of the Japanese sword and illustrate some of the uniquely Japanese innovations in the actual manufacture of the sword blade. The original iron-working technology imported from China was quickly adopted by native Japanese metalworkers and improved upon so that by the middle of the ninth century the process of combining different quality steels of controlled carbon content to produce a blade of complex cross-welded laminate construction was already well established.

The iron ore available to metalworkers was in the form known as *satetsu*, an ore-bearing sand found predominantly at sources near the coastal routes between Kyūshū and the main island of Honshū, in what are the modern-day prefectures of Hiroshima and Okayama. Ore used today is mainly from the Shimane region of Japan. The earliest Japanese smelters used in the production of iron from this ore were relatively small and were probably only able to produce modest quantities of the raw steel (*tamahage*) required for the manufacture of blades. It was not until later in the historical period that larger scale furnaces, *tatara*, came into being and were able to produce significant quantities of the raw material required to produce sword blades. However, the smelting process, ever since early times, involved the use of charcoal, a process which helped increase the purity and carbon content of the iron; this is a necessary requirement to produce raw steel, which is then further refined during the manufacture of the blade itself.

The Japanese sword blade is formed from a combination of two different steels, a harder, outer jacket of steel wrapped around a relatively softer, inner core of steel. This creates a blade with a hard, sharp cutting edge and an inner core which is resilient and able to absorb shocks in a way which reduces the possibility of the blade breaking or bending when used in combat. The *hadagane*, or outer skin of the blade, is produced by heating a block of high quality raw steel, with a relatively high carbon content, which is then hammered out into a bar. This is then cooled and broken up into smaller blocks which are checked for further impurities and then reassembled and reforged. During this process the billet of steel is heated and hammered, split and folded back upon itself many times and re-welded to create a complex structure of many thousands of layers. The precise way in which the steel is folded, hammered and re-welded determines the distinctive grain pattern of the blade, the *jihada* (also called *jigane* when referring to the actual surface of the steel blade), a feature which can be indicative of the period, place of manufacture and actual maker of the blade.

The *shingane* (or inner core of the blade) is of a relatively softer steel with a lower carbon content than the hadagane. For this, the block is again hammered, folded and welded in a similar fashion to the hadagane, but with a fewer number of folds. The hadagane block is once again heated, hammered out and folded into a 'U' shape, into which the shingane is inserted to a point just short of the tip. The new composite steel billet is then heated and hammered out ensuring that no air or dirt is trapped between the two layers of steel. The bar increases in length during this process until it approximates the final size and shape of the finished sword blade. A triangular section is cut off from the tip of the bar and shaped to create what will be the kissaki. At this point in the process, the blank for the blade is of rectangular section. This rough shape is referred to as a *sunobe* (plate 2).

The sunobe is again heated, section by section and hammered to create a shape which has many of the recognizable characteristics of the finished blade. These are a thick back (*mune*), a thinner edge (*ha*), a curved tip (*kissaki*), and notches on the edge (*hamachi*) and back (*munemachi*) which separate the blade from the tang (*nakago*). Details such as the ridge line (*shinogi*), another distinctive characteristic of the Japanese sword, are added at this stage of the process. The smith's skill comes in to play at this point, as the hammering process causes the blade to naturally curve in an erratic way, the thicker back tending to bend towards the thinner edge, and he must skilfully control the shape to give it the required upward curvature. The sunobe is finished by a process of filing and scraping which leaves all the physical characteristics and shapes of the blade recognizable. The surface of the blade is left in a relatively rough state, ready for the hardening processes. The sunobe is then covered all over with a clay mixture which is applied more thickly along the back and sides of the blade than along the edge. The blade is left to dry while the smith prepares the forge for the final heat treatment of the blade, the *yaki-ire*, the hardening of the cutting edge (plate 3).

This process takes place in a darkened smithy, usually at night, in order that the smith can judge by eye the colour and therefore the temperature of the sword as it is repeatedly passed through the glowing charcoal. When the time is deemed right (traditionally the blade should be the colour of the moon in February and August, which are the two months that appear most commonly on dated inscriptions on the nakago of the Japanese sword), the blade is plunged edge down and point forward into a tank of water. The precise time taken to heat the sword, the temperature of the blade and of the water into which it is plunged are all individual to each smith and they have generally been closely guarded secrets. Legend tells of a particular smith who cut off his apprentice's

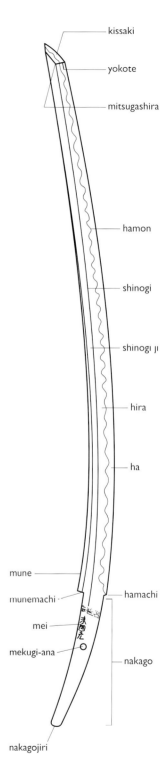

2 Line drawing of sword configuration.

3 In a darkened smithy the swordsmith heats a sunobe to the required temperature prior to the crucial yaki-ire process.

Photograph by Gregory Irvine.

4 A sword polisher, as depicted in the anonymous, 18th-century, woodblock-printed book *Shokunin Uta Awase* (Poetry Competition on the Theme of Craftsmen), which illustrates many scenes of artisans at work. V&A: E.2705–1925.

hand for testing the temperature of the water he used for the hardening process. In the different schools of sword makers there are many subtle variations in the materials used in the various processes and techniques outlined above, specifically in the form of clay applied to the blade prior to the yaki-ire, but all follow the same general procedures.

The application of the clay in different thicknesses to the blade allows the steel to cool more quickly along the thinner coated edge when plunged into the tank of water and thereby develop into the harder form of steel called martensite, which can be ground to razor-like sharpness. The thickly coated back cools more slowly retaining the pearlite steel characteristics of relative softness and flexibility. The precise way in which the clay is applied, and partially scraped off at the edge, is a determining factor in the formation of the shape and features of the crystalline structure known as the *hamon*. This distinctive tempering line found near the edge of the Japanese blade is one of the main characteristics to be assessed when examining a blade.

The martensitic steel which forms from the edge of the blade to the hamon is in effect the transition line between two different forms of steel, martensite and pearlite, and is where most of the shapes, colours and beauty in the steel of the Japanese sword are to be found. The variations in the form and structure of the hamon are all indicative of the period, smith, school or place of manufacture of the sword. As well as the aesthetic qualities of the hamon, there are, perhaps not unsurprisingly, real practical functions. The hardened edge is where most of any potential damage to the blade will occur in battle. This hardened edge is capable of being reground and sharpened many times, although the process will alter the shape of the blade.

When the blade has cooled, the clay is carefully removed and an intensive examination of the sword is carried out by the smith. Not all blades can physically survive this final hardening process and the smith examines the sword for minute flaws such as cracks, which would render the blade useless as a weapon, and assesses the aesthetic details such as the hamon which, if not defined clearly, would be displeasing to look at. The heating and quenching process also has the effect of naturally increasing the curve of the sword blade. This curvature can be corrected, if it is not to the smith's liking, through a hammering process. If, however, the sword does not satisfy all these requirements, it can be gently heated to return the blade to its original pearlite steel structure and the yaki-ire process can be repeated once again. Once the sword has been accepted, the smith will usually give it a rudimentary polish which cleans the lines of the blade, emphasizes the ridge-line and gives an initial sharpness to the edge. The sword is then passed to an expert polisher who, through a series of carefully graded polishing stones, will reveal the beauty of the structure of the blade (plate 4).

What is revealed through this polishing process are the crystalline structures which are formed during the hardening process and which have to a certain extent been pre-determined, or at least hoped for, by the smith through his control of the various stages of the forging procedures. The crystalline structures are in the main around or in the hamon and consist of martensite particles which are either individually invisible to the naked eye (*nioi*) or larger individually discernible crystals (*nie*). *Nioi* literally means 'fragrance' and is a rather poetic term for their smoke-like appearance in the hamon. They have also been described as appearing like the stars in the Milky Way. Nioi generally define the actual shape of the hamon. *Nie* means 'boiling' and these crystals can be found in varying patterns within the structure of the hardened edge of the blade. They can also be further defined as *ko-nie* (fine nie) or *ara-nie* (coarse nie).

The shape of the hamon formed by the nioi crystals has to a large extent already been predetermined by the way in which the smith applied the clay prior to the yaki-ire. The variation in the number of hamon patterns is almost limitless and the terminology used to describe them is extensive and far from an exact science (plate 5). The earliest swords had a simple straight hamon (*suguha*), while later swords developed irregularly undulating forms (*midareba*), wavy forms (*notare*), clove-flower-like forms (*chōjiba*) and many others, some with fantastic shapes, but all classified within the nomenclature.

Some swords display a feature described as *utsuri*, 'reflection'. This whitish pattern, which seems to reflect the hamon between the hamon itself and the shinogi, is created under special conditions of steel composition together with specific ways of heating the steel sunobe during the final hardening process. It does not, however, contain any martensite steel. The hamon extends into the kissaki of the blade and this portion is called the *boshi* (cap). There are fewer variations within this form than in the main part of the hamon, and the boshi can be straight or can turn back in a number of forms onto the back of the blade, but rarely travelling back further than the kissaki itself.

Although nie crystals are to be found within the hamon, they are more generally found in particular types of patterns near the hamon. These include the dense horizontal lines of nie crystals called *inazuma* (lightning), *kinsuji* (golden lines) and *sunagashi* (drifting sands). There are also vertical lines called *ashi* (legs) which stretch from the hamon to the edge of the blade. These have a practical function, as well as an aesthetic one, in that they potentially limit any chipping of the blade to an area between two ashi. Nie is also to be found on the main ground of the blade (*ji-nie*) either in individual darker patches such as *jifu* (ground spots) or as the descriptive *namazu hada* (catfish skin).

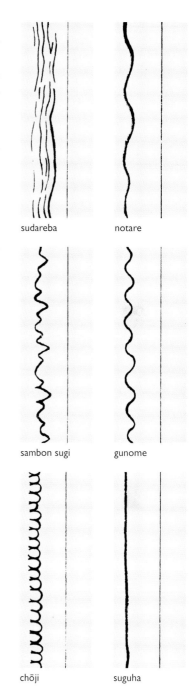

sudareba   notare

sambon sugi   gunome

chōji   suguha

5 Line drawings of hamon.

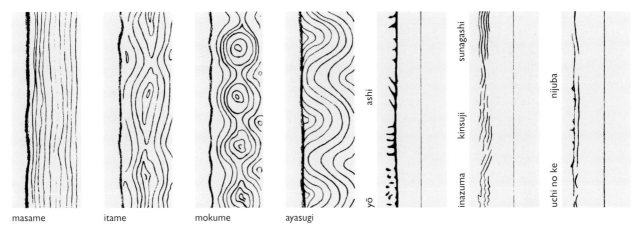

masame   itame   mokume   ayasugi   ashi   yō   inazuma   kinsuji   sunagashi   uchi no ke   nijuba

6 Line drawings of hada and nie.

7 Woodblock print entitled 'Inariyama Ko-Kaji' (The Swordsmith on Mount Inari) by Ogata Gekkō from the series entitled *Gekkō Zuihitsu* (Miscellaneous Sketches by Gekkō), *c.*1887. The print depicts Munechika forging the blade 'Ko-Kitsune' (Little Fox) assisted by Inari, the Shintō deity regarded as the guardian of smiths and metal workers. An ethereal group of foxes (the earthly messengers or manifestations of Inari) are in the background, and above the smith Munechika is a sacred rice-straw rope (shimenawa) with sacred paper (gohei) attached.
V&A: E.355–1901.

In some schools of sword manufacture nie is found in lines which follow the actual grain of the blade (plate 6).

The grain of the blade (*jihada*) produced through the forging process takes many forms, all having names associated with that of describing wood. Longitudinal grain is *masame*, burl grain is *mokume*, wood-grain – i.e. cut against the grain – is *itame*, while *ayasugihada* resembles the grain of the cryptomeria tree. The finest mokume grain is called *nashiji-hada*, and resembles the skin of the Japanese pear. Many swords do not conform to simply one particular form of jihada, and there can be combinations of any of the above in varying degrees and sizes. The actual colour and texture of the steel used in swords (*jitetsu*) can also vary considerably from bright to dark and velvety steel. As with the hamon, the type of steel, together with the resulting grain pattern, used to produce the Japanese sword can be indicative of period, smith, school and place of manufacture.

Traditionally the forging of a Japanese sword took place in near-religious conditions. The smithy would be purified by a Shintō priest and would have a sacred rice-straw rope (*shimenawa*), with sacred paper (*gohei*) attached as symbols of purity, erected to surround the smithy. Under no circumstances were women allowed to enter the smithy. The work of the smith could be seen as almost magical, as his sword-making techniques involved mastery over fire and metal. The smith (together with his assistants) would purify himself in mind and body through abstaining from eating meat, through sexual abstinence and through prayer. For the actual forging of the blade he would wear court robes or those of a Shintō priest. He may also continue to purify himself throughout the forging process by way of the customary Shintō purification ritual of cold water ablutions.

His prayers would invoke Buddhist deities as well as the Shintō deity Inari, god of rice and of metalworkers, who would often appear in the guise of a white fox. The famous Heian-period swordsmith Sanjō Munechika is said to have received personal assistance through the divine intervention of Inari when forging the blade Ko-Kitsune (Little Fox) for the Emperor Ichijō (r. 987–1011) (plate 7). The sword belonging to Minamoto Yoshitsune (1159–89) is believed to have been forged by a smith who invoked the name of Amida Buddha with every stroke of his hammer. As mentioned in the introduction, Japanese blades are thought to be imbued with a spirit which reflects the manner in which they have been forged, and can also be regarded as the physical manifestation of a kami.

2 | Development in the Heian Period
AD 794–1185

With the transfer of the Japanese imperial court from Nara to Heiankyo (modern-day Kyoto) in 794 by the Emperor Kammu, there was a slackening of ties with China, as Japan consolidated those political and religious philosophies it had earlier so readily adopted. This marked the beginning of the Heian period, a time referred to as the flowering of Japanese culture when the literary and aristocratic pursuits of the court reigned supreme.

The emperor being polygamous, it had long been customary for the lesser (or surplus) members of the imperial family to have their titles removed in the practice known as 'dynastic shedding'. This practice was intended to prevent disputes over accession rights. The surnames Taira and Minamoto were allocated to these superfluous aristocrats and they were sent to the remote provinces to govern in the emperor's name, thereby in principle strengthening his hold on an otherwise still unstable country. These two branches of the imperial line became the main protagonists in the disputes which later raged throughout the Heian period. Some, of course, preferred to stay in Kyoto, the centre of power and of the niceties of court life, leaving the real administration to their own appointees, but many others, seeking opportunities for advancement, took up the challenge and moved to the provinces.

By the year 792 the imperial court had abandoned its previous policy of conscription of the peasantry and left the organization of peace-keeping in the hands of a highly trained local militia, the *kondei*, a group of young officers chosen from among the eminent families of the court. The kondei were all but disbanded by the middle of the tenth century when groups of warriors known as *bushidan*, with loyalties based on kinship, especially to the Taira and Minamoto, began to evolve in the provinces, particularly in the eastern and northern Kantō region. The bushidan were a form of military gentry and they tended to be maintained as a fighting unit only so long as a military campaign required, their members returning to their farmlands as soon as possible after fighting.

The Japanese sword as we know it today, with its deep, graceful curve, developed sometime around the middle of the Heian period to service the need of this growing military class. Its shape reflected the changing form of warfare in Japan. Cavalry were now the predominant fighting unit and the older straight chokutō were particularly unsuitable for fighting from horseback. The curved sword is a far more efficient weapon when wielded by a warrior on horseback, where the curve of the blade adds considerably to the downward force of a cutting action.

Perhaps the earliest recorded (and extant) example of a sword with a deliberately forged curve is the blade known as Kogarasu Maru, the 'Little Crow' (plate 8). This sword, presently in the collection of the Japanese Imperial Household, formerly

8 Early Heian-period tachi blade known as the 'Kogarasu Maru' (Little Crow) and regarded as an excellent example of the transition between the straight chokutō and the curved sword. The Kogarasu Maru is reputed to have been made by the legendary smith Amakuni and was an heirloom of the Taira family. The blade is basically in kissaki-moroha style with central grooves on both sides and has a long, two-edged section with an overall even curvature and a deeper curve near the hilt.

Imperial Collections, Gyobutsu (Imperial Properties).

belonged to a member of the Taira clan. It is believed to have been forged by the semi-legendary smith known as Amakuni who was said to have lived in Yamato province during the eighth century. It is in kissaki-moroha style with an extremely long, sharpened upper edge which extends nearly halfway back along the blade. What distinguishes this sword from other chokutō which are in the kissaki-moroha style is the deep curve of the blade near the nakago together with a slight curve along the length of the blade itself. The other distinctive example of an intentionally curved blade to appear at this time was the *kenuki gata tachi* – 'tweezer-shaped tachi' – a form of sword which was to remain intermittently popular at court for centuries. In this sword the hilt is cut through with a longitudinal slot, the function of which is unclear, but may have been a device to absorb some of the shock received by the sword when cutting.

Technological developments had already much improved the manufacture of the swords of the Heian period, specifically with regard to the hardness of the steel. There were also significant improvements and advances in the forging techniques and final heat treatment for tempering of the blades. The shinogi, which was evident in the earlier katakiri-ha style of sword, is now to be found on both sides of the blade. The shinogi was moved away from the middle of the sword and nearer to the back, producing a blade which in cross-section looks not unlike a Gothic arch. This structure greatly increases the strength of the blade and gives a more acute angle to the hard cutting edge which is in turn supported by the thicker back and more flexible inner core of the blade.

The main features of the swords of the Heian period are the distinctive curve of the blade, predominantly near the hilt, in what is termed *koshi-zori* – 'waist' curve – with the upper part of the blade almost straight. The swords are long, slender and elegant, in combination with the characteristic called *fumbari*, where the width of the sword increases suddenly at the base of the blade adjacent to the hilt. The kissaki of Heian swords are generally small with a fairly straight edge and in this form are ideally suited to finding gaps in an enemy's armour. The sword was used mainly from horseback for slashing and a good sword in the hands of an experienced warrior would be quite capable of cutting through armour, including the helmet. The hamon of these blades are mostly straight, although there are gentle irregular undulations, midareba, to be found on some swords. The jihada of the blades are mostly masame or itame, which are occasionally found mixed.

The establishment of the 'Five Traditions'

The swords manufactured in and around Nara, the site of the former capital, were produced by smiths who eventually formed the Yamato school of swordsmiths. In the new capital of Kyoto itself, as well as in the surrounding countryside, the Yamashiro school of swordsmiths developed, and by the twelfth century new and distinctive characteristics of several other individual regional schools were beginning to emerge. These schools would eventually form the Gokaden, the 'Five Traditions of Japanese Sword Manufacturers', which were to dominate the world of the Japanese sword for hundreds of years. This term is particularly applicable to what are referred to as *kotō*, 'old swords', an expression which pertains to those swords produced from the Heian period up until approximately 1600; the precise end-date varies depending on the particular authority chosen. Within the Gokaden, subsidiary schools developed, usually based within one specific geographical area, but sometimes linked to individual master swordsmiths who may have moved from one province to another taking their individual characteristics of sword production with them (plate 9).

The Yamato school of Nara has the longest pedigree of all the schools and its work is characterized by a restrained and classical elegance. The manufacture of early Yamato blades is closely identified with the many old Buddhist temples of Nara. The precise form of the early blades is unclear, but certainly by the end of the Heian period the recognizable characteristics of the school's blades had become well established with suguha hamon of fine nioi, occasionally combined with a midareba hamon and jihada of masame or itame. The swords of the Yamato school tended to be thicker at the shinogi, giving a less acute cutting edge. The semi-legendary swordsmith Amakuni, maker of the Kogarasu Maru, was believed to have lived in the province of Yamato during the eight century. Also by the end of the Heian period considerable numbers of blades were being produced for the powerful and militant Buddhist monasteries (such as those at Tōdaiji in Nara itself), which maintained sizeable armies to fight other monasteries and provincial warlords for imperial favours.

While there had been swordsmiths in and around Kyoto since the time of the imperial court's transfer from Nara, the Yamashiro school as a recognizable entity is regarded as having been founded some time during the twelfth century by Sanjō Munechika. Being swords produced principally to meet the requirements of the aristocrats (and military guards) of the imperial court, the blades of the Yamashiro school are characterized by an extreme elegance and graceful curvature. It has been said that, beginning with the swords of the Yamashiro school,

9 Heian-period (11th century) tachi blade with the faint signature of 'Yasutsuna' (Yasutsuna of Hōki Province). Considered one of the five best blades in Japan, it was used, according to legend, by Minamoto Yorimitsu to kill the monster Shuten Dōji (probably a fierce brigand) – hence its name 'Dōjigiri'. The blade is in its original form, having never been cut down, and was reputedly successively owned by Oda Nobunaga, Toyotomi Hideyoshi and Tokugawa Ieyasu. Collection of the Tokyo National Museum, National Treasure.

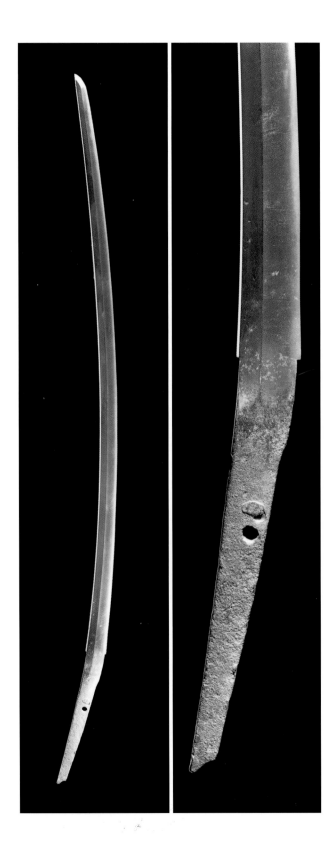

the Japanese sword was transformed from a simply functional weapon to one which combined beauty of structure with elegance of form, as well as being a most efficient cutting weapon.

Munechika's own blades have small kissaki, deep koshi-zori and strong fumbari, which has perhaps at times been somewhat exaggerated by the repeated polishing the blades have endured over the centuries. Their jihada is ko-itame and the hamon has combined nie and nioi with a tendency towards midareba. A distinctive characteristic of his work is the crescent moon-like shapes found in the hamon of his blades, notably on the sword known as Mikazuki (Quarter Moon), which was probably named thus after this style of hamon, rather than the shape of the actual sword (plate 10). His blades are somewhat rare, but were an essential possession for members of the great families. This desirability, coupled with rarity, led to many fakes being produced, or instances of Munechika's signature being added to swords of dubious provenance. The production of fakes and forgeries, and the historical appraisal and appreciation of swords, particularly *meitō* – famous, or named swords – will be discussed later in the book.

The most prolific producers of swords within the Gokaden were the schools of the province of Bizen, modern-day Okayama prefecture. Bizen had long been a major centre for iron production, having iron ore in plenty, mostly in the form of satetsu. Within Bizen itself the main centre of manufacture was the town of Osafune, where there were significant numbers of swordsmiths who began from this time to include the name of Osafune on the inscriptions on the nakago of their swords together with their own names. Of note among the other early smiths from Bizen are Kanehira and Masatsune who also produced elegant blades.

10 Tachi blade known as 'Mikazuki Munechika' (Quarter-Moon Munechika). The omote bears the faint signature 'Sanjō' (Sanjō Munechika) and is one of the genuine works by one of the greatest of the late Heian-period swordsmiths. The elegant shape and fine steel structure and details of the blade have justly qualified it for inclusion in the 'Tenka Gōken' (Five Greatest Swords Under Heaven).
Collection of the Tokyo National Museum,
Gift of Mr Watanabe Seiichiro, National Treasure.

Early Bizen blades have a distinctive koshi-zori curvature, fumbari and a small kissaki. Their jihada are generally itame and the hamon are strong in ko-nie and of *ko-midare* (gently undulating) form. More unusual styles of hamon began to develop within the Bizen school of sword makers, notably the introduction of the *chōji* hamon. This pattern has the appearance of a line of tightly bunched buds of clove (*chōji*) flowers. Another distinctive introduction was that of utsuri, a style of patterning particularly associated with the Bizen schools from the late Heian period onwards. These attributes are all to be found in the blades of Tomonari. Later blades produced at Osafune tended to have less of a koshi-zori curve as the curve of the blade became more even and moved nearer the centre of the blade in what is called *torii-zori*. This describes the similarity of the blade's curvature to the upper crossbar of the gateway to a Shintō shrine, which is known as a Torii.

Sword mounting and decoration

Beginning in the Heian period, the surface of the blade was at times cut into for decorative or purely functional reasons. Simple grooves, generally above the shinogi, were cut in order to lighten or adjust the balance of the blade, but at the same time served to emphasize the elegant curvature of the blade. These grooves (*hi* or *bohi*) could be short, extending just a little way from the nakago for about 10 centimetres, or could stretch as far as the kissaki. Some were incised for the entire length of the blade, extending as far as the butt of the nakago. Some carvings (*horimono*) were both more decorative and more symbolic. For example, the Buddhist deity Fudō Myō-Ō was important for both warrior and swordsmith due to his ferocious attributes. He is often depicted standing surrounded by flames and holding a rope in one hand with which to bind the enemies of Buddhism, and in the other hand a *ken*, a double-edged sword with which to subdue the enemies of Buddhism. Small carvings of Fudō in this form, or stylized versions of his sword (*suken*), were sometimes cut into blades. His rope, in the form of a dragon, was also to be found carved into the blade where it is seen wrapped around the ken. Sometimes a debased Sanskrit character (*bonji*) for a warlike deity such as Fudō, Benten or Bishamonten would be inscribed on the blade, thereby carrying out the dual function of providing both protection and a sense of steadfast resolve for the warrior.

The tachi sword was worn slung on the left of the body with the cutting edge down and the hilt to the front. The signature on the nakago of the blade was inscribed in such a way that it would always be on the outside of the sword when worn. This characteristic is important in recognizing the development, function and different styles of wearing swords from this time onwards. The outer face of the nakago (when the sword is worn) is called the *omote*, the inner is the *ura*. When worn with full armour, the tachi would be accompanied by a shorter blade in the form known as *koshigatana* – 'waist sword' – a type of short sword with no hand-guard (*tsuba*), where the hilt and scabbard meet to form the style of mounting called an *aiguchi*, 'meeting mouth'. Daggers were also carried for close combat fighting as well as generally for personal protection, the *tantō* being the common term for this type of short-edged weapon. However, very few identifiable tantō or koshigatana blades from the Heian period exist today, and those which do have frequently been retempered and their original hamon lost.

11 Kazari-dachi (court sword), comprising a scabbard of nashiji lacquer with mother-of-pearl inlay (pairs of Hō-ō birds) and metal fittings of gold filigree work, late Heian period.
Collection of the Tokyo National Museum, National Treasure.

12 Hyōgo Gusari tachi, mounted in a metal-covered scabbard and suspended by chains. This elegant Kamakura-period tachi mounting bears a triple triangle crest design and is known as the Hōjo tachi.
Collection of the Tokyo National Museum, Important Cultural Property.

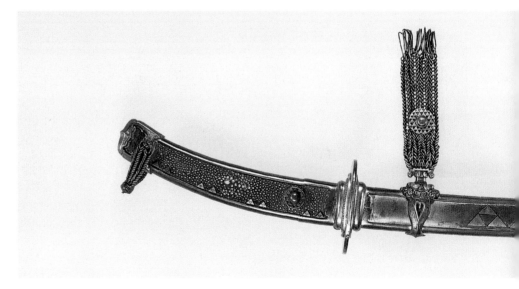

Sword mountings of the Heian period tend to fall into two distinct types: those for use at court and those for the military. Among the court-style mountings, the *kazari-dachi* was by far the most common, and this style remained in use until the nineteenth century. Being intended purely for ceremonial occasions and generally worn by courtiers rather than warriors, the kazari-dachi tended to hold a simple bar of iron, rather than an excellent forged steel blade. The decoration of these mountings, however, was luxurious and included finely worked gold and gilt-copper fittings

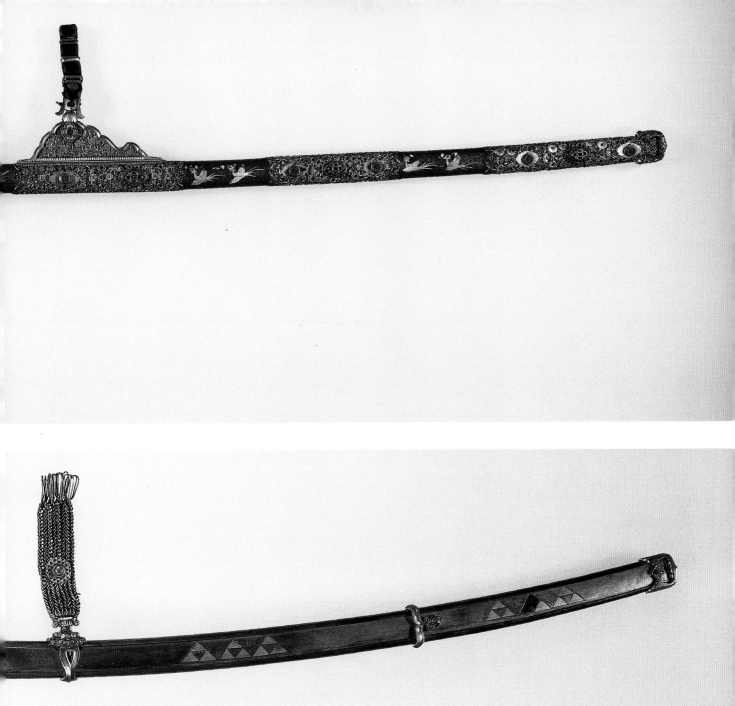

encrusted with jewels and semi-precious stones all mounted in sumptuously lacquered scabbards (plate 11).

The most common style of military mounting for the tachi at this time was the simple black scabbard, perhaps first wrapped in leather prior to lacquering, with plain metal fittings of copper or iron. The hilt of the tachi was wooden and wrapped in the hard-wearing skin of the rayfish (*same*), with a small decorative metal fitting, the *menuki*, added to give a better handgrip underneath the outer wrapping of leather or silk

13 Group of arrowheads, Edo period. These include simple types to pierce armour; a forked type (called *karimata* by Knutsen, *Japanese Polearms*) to cut through armour cords (or ropes) or bring down game birds; barbed types for hunting or to incapacitate an enemy; and a ceremonial spade-shaped arrowhead.

V&A: M.3–1909, M.13–1909, M.35–1916, M.954–1916, M.96–1919, M.402–1928, M.426–1928, M.442–1928, M.444–1928, M.456–1928, M.460–1928, M.467–1928.

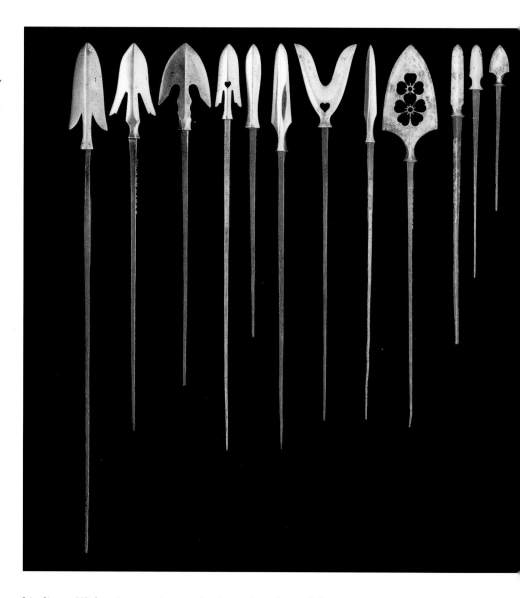

bindings. With minor variations in the styles of metal fittings, the method of tachi mounting established during the Heian period remained in use until the late nineteenth century and the abolition of the military class. Other military mountings of the Heian period include the *Hyōgo Gusari tachi*, an elegant tachi mounted in a metal-covered scabbard and suspended by chains (plate 12).

The unique style of the Japanese sword had by now evolved so far from the original mainland Asian forms that Japanese blades were renowned in China itself and were evidently being exported to mainland Asia. Ouyang Xiu, a Chinese scholar and official writing in the middle of the Song period (AD 960–1279) referred to them: 'Treasure swords of Japan are obtained from the East by merchants of Yue. Their scabbards are of fragrant wood, covered with shark skin; gold, silver, copper, and metals adorn them, hundreds of gold pieces is their cost. When wearing such a sword, one can slay the Barbarians.'[1]

While the sword was carried at all times into battle, it was in fact the bow which was the principle weapon of the mounted warrior. Provincial warriors, notably those in the northern Kantō, developed and mastered the art of warfare from horseback in 'the way of the horse and the bow' – *kyūba-michi* – a warrior tradition which was eventually to develop into the philosophical and practical martial concept of *Bushidō*, 'the Way of the Warrior'. The Japanese bow (*yumi*) is over 2 metres long with the grip one third of the way up from the bottom which enables the warrior to pass the bow more easily over the horse's head to aim and fire. The shafts of the arrows are long with a wide variety of steel arrowheads (*ya-no-ne*) in varying shapes with different functions (plate 13). The simplest arrowhead is designed to penetrate the lamellar armour which was worn from the Heian period onwards. Other forms were designed to cut through armour or make terrifying noises when fired. In action, the warrior stood up in the saddle on solid comma-shaped stirrups to aim and fire his bow or to cut down with his tachi.

A vivid description of a mounted warrior in battle comes from the eleventh-century 'Tales of Mutsu' – *Mutsuwaki* – written by a courtier and detailing the exploits of the Minamoto clan during the wars of sub-jugation of the native tribes of northern Japan. Describing Minamoto Yoshiie, the *Mutsuwaki* vividly illustrate his heroic actions thus: 'He fired arrows from horseback like a god. Undaunted by their dazzling blades he rushed through the enemies' ranks… With his great arrows he transfixed one enemy commander after another, never firing indiscriminately, but always inflicting a deadly wound' (plate 14).

By the eleventh century the *bushidan* had become a more permanent feudal entity, with relationships no longer necessarily based on blood ties. The lord and vassal relationship was perpetuated from generation to generation, the ties often being thought of in fictional kinship terms. For example, vassals were designated as children of the house (*ie-no-ko*), and lords looked up to as fathers. It became inevitable that over time a clearly defined military class developed, with their allegiance to local family groupings rather than with the remote court in Kyoto. It is from these allegiances to the regional feudal lords that the *samurai* – literally 'one who serves' – began to emerge as a distinct class. The term *bushi*, with a meaning of military gentry, is also applied to this distinct military class, and 'samurai' and 'bushi' are interchangeable words in the history of Japan's military class.

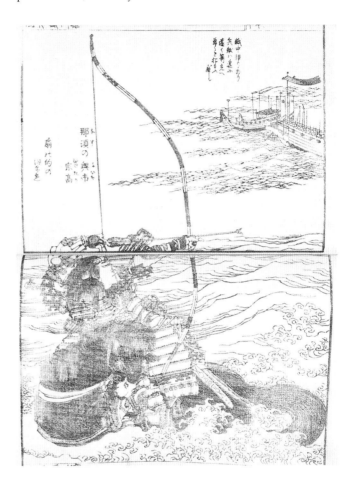

14 Print from *Ehon Musashi Abumi* (Picture Book of the Stirrups of Musashi), a woodblock-printed book by Katsushika Hokusai, 1836. The use of the bow is clearly demonstrated by the mounted warrior Nasu no Yoichi Munetake, a warrior of the Genji clan who famously shot through a fan held up by a warrior of the Heike clan at the Battle of Yashima in 1185. V&A: E.15071–1886.

3 | The Kamakura Period 1185–1333

The establishment of the samurai and the military government

Removed from the niceties of court life, the various clans in the provinces developed a fighting reputation as they strove to consolidate their own positions. The Minamoto established themselves as particularly great fighters, and so powerful was Minamoto no Yoshiie (1039–1106) that many of the lesser samurai families commended their lands to his protection. The court in Kyoto, however, fearing for their own safety, began to favour the Taira clan, who grew from strength to strength. In the mid-twelfth century there were two major political disturbances, both with their roots in questions of succession to the imperial throne and its control. In the first, the Hōgen Disturbance (1156), the Taira and Minamoto were on both sides of the fighting, but in the Heiji Disturbance of 1160 the two families were completely opposed to each other. From this latter dispute the Taira clan emerged as victors and under Taira no Kiyomori established themselves as the new military aristocracy in Kyoto, where they began to behave more like courtiers than warriors, and involved themselves in court politics.

The Minamoto, however, continued to consolidate and build upon their warrior heritage, and in a final nationwide conflict from 1180 to 1185 (the Gempei Wars; plate 15) the Minamoto inflicted a crushing defeat on the Taira clan at the Battle of Dan no Ura. During this conflict all major Taira leaders were killed, along with the child Emperor Antoku, grandson of Taira no Kiyomori, who is believed to have drowned along with the imperial regalia. In 1185 Minamoto no Yoritomo established his military government (*Bakufu*, 'tent government') at Kamakura. In 1192 Yoritomo was appointed *Shōgun* (an abbreviation of *Seii tai Shōgun*, 'Barbarian Conquering Generalissimo') by the Emperor Go-Toba, thereby beginning what was to become 700 years of effective military rule of Japan by various families who acted, at least nominally, in the name of the emperor in Kyoto.

On one level these wars could be seen as simply a clash between the two families of imperial descent vying for greater national political power than that which they had obtained in their allocated provincial domains. On another level the wars could be regarded as a revolution by the provincial landowning warriors against their aristocratic political rulers in Kyoto who had tried to impose their will from a distance. In many respects the individual aims of the Taira and Minamoto had much in common. Many of the lesser samurai families who sided with the Taira and Minamoto did not do so merely out of loyalty to these major clans, but saw the opportunity to establish firmer control over their own domains in allegiance with the military might of whichever of the two families they backed and who they hoped would be the eventual victor in the conflict.

The Kamakura period, being the beginning of the domination of the country by the

military class, is often referred to as the Golden Age of the Japanese sword, and
certainly this period produced many of the finest blades ever made. There were many
further technological advances, occurring mostly in and around Kamakura itself,
which rapidly developed from a small fishing village into the principal cultural and
administrative centre for the country. As the major military centre, Kamakura naturally
attracted, and indeed promoted, a great influx of swordsmiths from all over the realm
who brought with them the various traditions from their respective schools, notably
the Bizen, Yamato and Yamashiro traditions. In a very short period of time these
swordsmiths laid the foundations for what was to become the Sōshū, or Sagami,
tradition of sword makers, the fourth tradition of the Gokaden based in and around
Kamakura itself.

The Minamoto Bakufu under Yoritomo had consolidated their position with the creation of an impressive economic and political system of administration operating
through family and vassalage ties with land apportioned directly to family members and
to loyal followers. The Kamakura period was in reality one of authority divided between
the imperial court in Kyoto and the shōgun in Kamakura (although the actions of the
shōgun were nominally done in the name of the emperor). Although Yoritomo and his
successors tried to limit their authority to matters pertaining to the military, it was to the
shōgunate at Kamakura that the population turned for solutions to their problems. On
Yoritomo's death in 1199, his two sons took over the reins of government, but were little
more than figurehead shōguns, the real power lying with the powerful Hōjō family,
from whom Yoritomo's widow was descended. The Hōjō assumed power in 1219 following the assassination of the third Minamoto shōgun, Sanetomo. In 1221 the cloistered
Emperor Go-Toba (1180–1239, r.1183–98) attempted to overthrow the new Hōjō Bakufu,
but was defeated and sent into exile on the island of Oki. From this position he was able
to concentrate on his great love of swords, their manufacture and history.

From his exile he summoned eminent swordsmiths, together with the necessary professional sword polishers, to visit him on Oki for a fixed period during the year. These
craftsmen were given the title *Gōban Kaji*, 'Smiths in attendance to the emperor'. In
return for the imperial patronage, the smiths taught the emperor the many techniques
of the established Gokaden schools, particularly those of Bizen and Yamashiro. It is
believed that Go-Toba was actually involved in at least the yaki-ire process (of hardening the blades) but the precise extent of his involvement in any of the more arduous
tasks of forging the blades is not known (plate 16). It was regarded as a great honour to
work with the emperor, and blades produced by Go-Toba and his attendant smiths are
not signed, but bear the twenty-four-leaf imperial chrysanthemum crest on the nakago.
With this previously unheard of patronage, the Japanese sword gained even more
status as an art object during a period when its prime function, in the bloody and
violent state of the country, was as a killing instrument.

Of note among the Gōban Kaji was Norimune of Bizen province who is said to have
founded the Fukuoka Ichimonji school of swordsmiths. Later in the Kamakura period,
as a reward and sign of respect for the excellence of their blades, Go-Toba is said to have
awarded the school the privilege of signing their blades with the horizontal single character *Ichi*, 'Number one'. This is an abbreviated form of *Tenka Ichi*, 'First under heaven
[the realm]', and the school became known as the *Ichimonji*. Many of the blades which

bear the imperial crest are in the style of the older Bizen school, and the influence of Norimune and the other Bizen smiths among the Gōban Kaji on the styles of blades favoured by the emperor must have been substantial.

The Hōjō Bakufu continued the martial ethos established by Yoritomo, and a regime of strict military training was enforced by a legal code laid down in 1232 whereby the warrior class was instructed to study the military arts of horsemanship, archery and the sword. Smiths from all over the country continued to travel to Kamakura to join the ever-growing number of swordsmiths who were producing excellent blades for the military rulers. The tachi blades of the early part of the Kamakura period were little different to those of the Heian period and the established schools continued to flourish in the prevailing military atmosphere of the country. The demand for good functional blades was stronger than ever before.

The shape of the blade gradually began to alter, and the koshi-zori and fumbari of earlier types gave way to torii-zori blades of more even and deeper curve and with more consistent breadth. The shape of the kissaki did not change, but their appearance, combined with the newer shape of the blade gave them a 'stubbier' form, earning them the name of *ikubi* – bull-necked – *kissaki*. Blades of this period became thicker, specifically near the shinogi, and developed a more convex cross-section, or *hira*, which enabled the sword to cut more efficiently through armour. This type of gently convex hira is known as a *hamaguri ha*, 'clam blade'. These developments indicate a gradual change in the patterns of warfare at this time, as the sword was increasingly used over the bow and there was a gradual tendency towards closer and individual hand-to-hand combat in battle.

Up until this time warfare in Japan was rather disorganized, tending towards individual combat and large-scale skirmishes which were usually prefaced by a declaration of each of the protagonists' lineage (*ujibumi o yomu*). An example from the *Heike Monogatari*, the vivid war tales of the battles between the Taira and Minamoto, illustrates this well:

> Behold me! I am Mataro Tadatsuna, aged seventeen, the son of Ashikaga no Tarō Toshitsuna, tenth generation descendant of Tawara no Tōta Hidesato, a warrior who long ago won fame and rewards for destroying the enemies of the emperor... Here I stand, ready to meet any among the men of the third rank nyūdō![2]

Honour in battle was extremely important and it was necessary to establish the rank of an opponent in order to judge whether dishonour would result from the possibility of being killed by one of lower rank or status. There are several well-documented, although perhaps over romanticized, tales from the Taira-Minamoto wars of individuals refusing to give their names or ranks as they knew that their opponents were superior warriors, but were of lower rank.

Closer combat fighting in the Kamakura period resulted in the production of more tantō blades. These were mostly in the flat hira-zukuri style with slight uchi-zori, but two newer shapes developed which were more efficient at penetrating armour. One was the *kammuri-otoshi* – sloping 'crown' style – which has a strong curve near the tip, a shinogi but a thin mune which thickens abruptly in section approximately 10 centimetres from the munemachi. The other was the *u-no-kubi* – 'cormorant's neck' – which has a similar profile to the kammuri-otoshi but with a thick, diamond-section point which thins rapidly back to the place where the blade thickens again in a similar fashion to the kammuri-otoshi.

Pre-eminent among the makers of swords in the early thirteenth century were those of the Bizen tradition, particularly swordsmiths of the Ichimonji school. The hamon of the Ichimonji school were large, sometimes reaching almost to the shinogi, and flamboyant with large forms of chōji in unusual patterns. One such unusual pattern was *kawazu chōji*, where the tops of the chōji resembled the heads of tadpoles. The Bizen schools continued to produce blades with striking utsuri and hamon strong in nioi, in contrast to their earlier predominantly nie hamon. Osafune in Bizen remained a centre for the production of excellent blades, especially those from the three smiths given the appellation *sansaku*, 'the three makers'. These were Mitsutada, Nagamitsu and Sanenaga, who produced fine-grained blades with chōji hamon and distinctive boshi which swells away from the edge of the blade (plate 17).

The Yamashiro school was also active at this time, producing fine tachi blades with restrained chōji hamon in delicate ko-nie. Superb tantō were made by Yoshimitsu, whose hira-zukuri daggers are long and elegant with a restrained suguha hamon with slight midare, some *gunome* (abrupt swellings of the hamon) and much ko-nie. The Yamato schools continued to produce good, functional blades for the warrior monks, the *sōhei*. These blades are generally unsigned and feature strong masame hada, sometimes almost perfectly parallel graining. The kammuri-otoshi style of tantō was forged in considerable numbers by the Yamato schools.

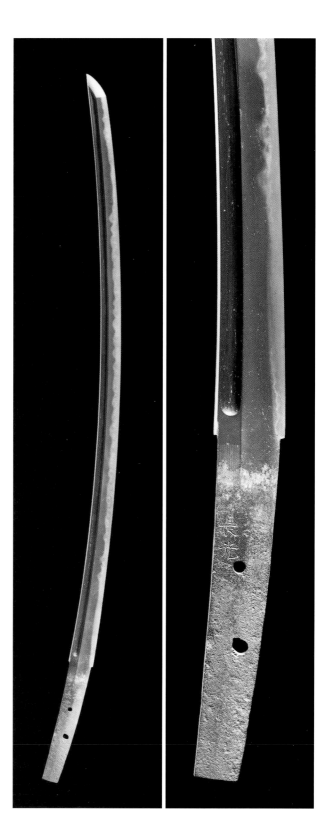

17 Tachi blade signed 'Nagamitsu' and known as the 'Dai Hannya Nagamitsu' after the Buddhist Dai Hannya Sutra. Nagamitsu of Osafune in Bizen was one of the Kamakura-period *sankaku*, 'three makers'. The blade is suriage but still shows the deep curve typical of Kamakura-period blades and also displays some of the utsuri found on Bizen blades of this period.
Collection of the Tokyo National Museum, National Treasure.

18 Woodblock print from the book, *Ehon Zen Taiheiki*, showing the effective use of naginata by foot soldiers against mounted warriors. The weapons and armour of the period are also realistically depicted, with all the combatants carrying tachi and koshigatana. This anonymous, 18th-century book, whose title translates as 'Chronicle of the Great Peace', reflecting perhaps the author's desire for more peaceful times, illustrates stories from the anonymous *gunki monogatari* (war tales), which describe the conflict raging in Japan during the period 1318–67. V&A: E.14979–1886.

The Mongol invasions and their consequences

Among the most significant events of the middle Kamakura period were the unsuccessful invasions of the Mongols under Kublai Khan in 1274 and 1281. These invasions were stopped by the *Kamikaze*, the Divine Wind which on both occasions destroyed the Mongol invasion fleet, but not until after the Mongols had devastated areas of western Japan and had forced the Japanese armies to retreat. The Japanese cavalry was completely thrown by the Mongol's use of massed archery, exploding bombs and crashing cymbals which terrified the Japanese horses, and by the hordes of Mongol infantry armed with large spears and other polearms. The Mongols, unsurprisingly, had little time for the etiquette of battle which the Japanese had traditionally observed.

These two unsuccessful invasions had several consequences. One was the partial destabilization of the Hōjō Bakufu which had proved to be ill-prepared for such events and had afterwards failed to reward, or recognize, the efforts of those who had defended the country so well, causing resentment and dissatisfaction. The other consequence was a major shift in Japanese battle tactics from predominantly cavalry to infantry, together with the development of larger types of swords and an increase in the production of spears (*yari*) and halberds (*naginata*). Naginata and yari had been used as far back as the Heian period, but no positively identifiable blades from this period exist today. The naginata features prominently in the illustrated handscrolls which depict the wars of the Taira and Minamoto graphically and in great detail. It is from these scrolls that we have a good idea of how the various weapons of the period were used in battle (plate 18). Unusually, and despite the Mongols effective use of their shorter bows in massed formation, the physical configuration of the Japanese bow and the way it was used on the battlefield remained basically unchanged.

Japan remained on war-readiness for a considerable period of time after these invasions and the production of swords generally increased. In Kamakura itself the Sagami, or Sōshū, school of swordsmiths became fully established under Shintōgo Kunimitsu. Kunimitsu was, depending on which of several written lineages are consulted, the son or pupil of Awataguchi Kunitsuna, who in 1249 was summoned from Kyoto by the Hōjō regent, Tokiyori, to forge a tachi blade. What is known from dated blades is that Kunimitsu was certainly working from 1293 until 1334 (plate 19). The Sagami school in the Kamakura period is renowned for its tantō blades, and nowhere was the excellence of these blades better seen than in the work of Masamune, one of the pupils of Kunimitsu.

Masamune is generally regarded as the greatest swordsmith in the history of the Japanese sword. His blades, mostly tantō, were both strong and beautiful and could cut extremely efficiently. He devised ways of improving the forging techniques, and the jihada of his weapons reflects the complicated combination of different steels used in their production. This is evidenced by the copious amounts of nie found in the blades, characteristically

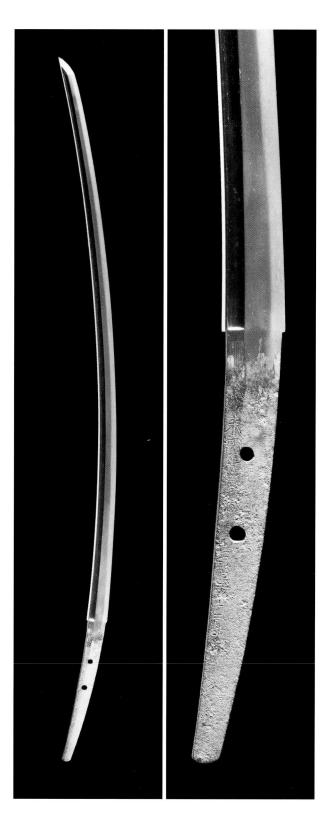

19 Tachi blade signed 'Rai Kunimitsu' and 'Kanreki ni nen, ni gatsu, hi' (a day in the second month of the second year of the Kanreki period [equivalent to 1327]). Kunimitsu of the Rai group of Yamashiro swordsmiths created robust yet elegant blades with broad suguha and slight midare hamon and with ko-itame jihada.

Collection of the Tokyo National Museum, National Treasure.

ji-nie – nie on the ground of the blade – which are to be found in the lines of bright nie called *chikei*. The hamon of Masamune's blades are mostly notare with sections in midareba. Also to be observed within Masamune's hamon are the distinctive nie features of individual graining called *kinsuji* (golden lines), found in irregular horizontal lines parallel to the edge of the blade, and *inazuma* (lightning), zigzag lines at angles to the edge of the blade. Both of these features are bright streaks of martensitic steel imbedded in the pearlitic body of the blade. *Sunagashi* (drifting sands) are also found, and these are similar to kinsuji but are more regular and thicker lines of nie (plate 20).

Most of the technological advances accredited to Masamune were extremely practical ones brought about by experience gained during the recent battles against the Mongols. Many blades had been damaged during the severe fighting and had broken or chipped right through the tempered edge, past the hamon and into the softer untempered section of the blade. This rendered the blade useless, as damage past the tempered edge meant that it could no longer be re-ground and used again as a practical sword. Masamune was able to manufacture blades with a wider tempered edge, which meant that, if damaged, the blade could be re-ground many times at the edge before the softer steel was reached. The changes in the styles of warfare brought about by the two Mongol invasions meant that hand-to-hand combat by individuals became ever more commonplace. The fine tantō produced by Masamune (and others) at that time fulfilled this new requirement for battle, and Masamune's sword-manufacturing techniques were studied and copied by many other smiths.

Although he was to have a great influence on the future of sword making all over Japan, there are actually few signed blades by Masamune. Various theories have been put forward to explain this fact. An early treatise on meitō explains the lack of signed blades by stating that, as Masamune's work was so distinctive, there was no need for him to sign his blades. One nineteenth-century theory went so far as to suggest that due to the rarity of signed blades there was a possibility that Masamune did not exist at all. A perhaps more acceptable theory is that as a direct servant of the shōgun in Kamakura he was commissioned to produce blades and therefore a signature was not necessary, perhaps even presumptuous considering the status of his client. The few tachi produced by Masamune were extremely long and in later centuries were shortened to suit the different styles of combat of those periods. This shortening process potentially removed any extant signature, although there was in later years a practice of inlaying signatures in gold into the nakago of shortened blades.

The extensive requirements of the military families for good quality arms and armour and the continual campaigning during the Kamakura period are reflected in the production of what are generally regarded as some of the best swords in Japanese history. In particular, the schools of Bizen excelled, and it is from Bizen that we find many excellent blades with not only the smith's name inscribed on the nakago, but the province, town and date of manufacture, a tradition which was to continue throughout the history of the Japanese sword. The production of weapons was given an added impetus when in 1333, following the years of dissatisfaction with the Hōjō Bakufu after the Mongol invasions, various provincial military rulers (*Shugo*), originally appointed by the Kamakura Bakufu, rose in open warfare against the regime and Kamakura itself was stormed and set ablaze. The country was set for an extended period of civil war.

The main cause for this uprising was the fact that the Emperor Go-Daigo had refused to abdicate in favour of a Hōjō-backed emperor. In 1333 Ashikaga Takauji, the head of a powerful branch of the Minamoto family, was sent against Go-Daigo, but defected and assisted him in attacking the Hōjō. Other eastern families rose up and within several days Kamakura was devastated. Go-Daigo returned the seat of power to Kyoto, but within three years Ashikaga Takauji had rebelled against the court-based policies of Go-Daigo and set up his own warrior-backed rival emperor in the north of Kyoto with Go-Daigo fleeing south to Yoshino.

20 Tachi blade known as 'Kanze Masamune', Kamakura period, early 14th century. This heavily cut-down blade bears all the characteristics of the work of Masamune of the Sōshū tradition, notably the broad notare hamon with its horizontal lines of nie in sunagashi and kinsuji. Any original inscriptions would have been lost with the shortening of the blade to uchigatana style. The extent of the shortening can be seen from the fact that the horimono (much polished away) is now almost entirely in the nakago. The blade was named after the great family of Tokugawa-sponsored Nō actors, the Kanze, who owned the blade for some time.

Collection of the Tokyo National Museum, National Treasure.

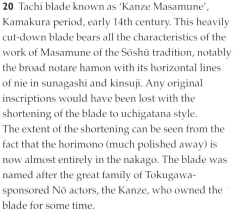
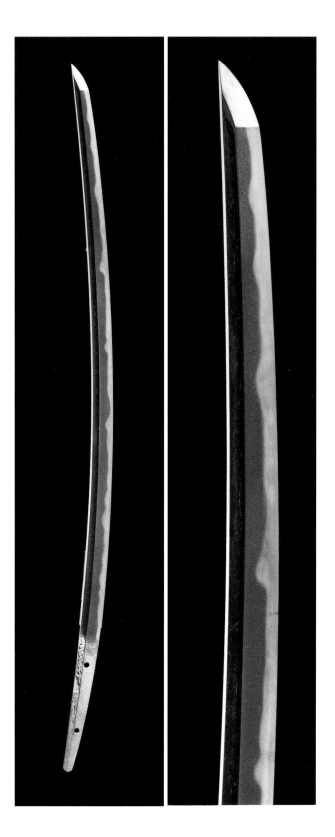

4 | The Muromachi and Momoyama Periods
1333–1600

The Nambokuchō period

The ensuing sixty-year period is called the Nambokuchō, or the Southern and Northern Courts period. During this time civil war raged throughout the country, but particularly in and around Kyoto itself and the moors of Yoshino. The wars continued until 1392 when Ashikaga Yoshimitsu and his warrior-supported northern dynasty emerged as victors. The Ashikaga family had assumed the title of shōgun and set up the base for their own Bakufu in the Muromachi area of Kyoto, from which the period derives its name. The extended warfare revived the martial spirit of the country and ever more increasingly it was carried out by warriors on foot.

Accordingly, many swords made during the Nambokuchō period reflected the primary importance of the cutting power of the blade when wielded by a foot soldier. Swords became longer and heavier and with larger kissaki. One specific type of sword, the *nodachi*, became briefly popular and was especially effective against cavalry as it had a cutting length of a metre or more. These swords were far too long to be carried at the waist and drawn from this position, and so were slung across the back and frequently mounted in disposable scabbards of paper or straw. Very few of these blades survive today as they were cut down to a more manageable length by successive owners. Some are found in their original configuration in Shintō shrines where they were donated as votive offerings (plate 21).

Other swords of this period continued to follow the earlier Kamakura style of leather mountings, which were rugged, waterproof and ideally suited to long periods of campaigning. There was, however, the introduction of a new and distinctive form of mounting for the tachi. This was the *ito-maki no tachi*, where the area of the lacquered scabbard between the two suspension links was wrapped in silk braiding to prevent damage to the scabbard, which at this point would otherwise rub against armour (plates 22 and 23).

The daggers which had become more common during the later Kamakura period continued to be produced in considerable numbers as the requirement for weapons for hand-to-hand combat was increasingly of prime importance. One unusual form of dagger, the *mete zashi*, had a pronounced curve at the hilt, was worn on the right side with the cutting edge forward and could be drawn quickly in close combat to drive upwards into the weaker spots of an opponent's armour. Daggers of the period were mostly long and broad with an even curve to the blade. Large numbers of polearms also continued to be produced and the naginata blades of the Nambokuchō period were often of considerable length, sometimes up to one metre; when mounted on long poles, they became a most effective weapon (plate 24). They were particularly popular with members of the militant Buddhist clergy, the sōhei. Naginata-type blades were also

21 Suriage katana blade, unsigned. This heavily cut down blade shows many of the characteristics of the large swords produced during the Nambokuchō period.
The blade was a gift from the city of Kagoshima to Sir Claude MacDonald, British Ambassador to Japan from 1905 to 1912.
V&A: M.137–1929, MacDonald Gift.

22 Ito-maki no tachi with the scabbard decorated in gold nashiji lacquer with *kiri-mon* and *karakusa* scrolling. The metal fittings are all by the Gotō school and are of shakudō inlaid with gold. The section of the scabbard near the suspension cords is wrapped with silk brocades to prevent the expensive lacquer from being abraded when the sword is worn with full armour. This mounting, for a 14th-century sword, was probably assembled around 1850 (see plate 23 for the blade).
V&A: M.139–1929, MacDonald Gift.

mounted on shorter handles and were described as *nagamaki*. These were used more as swords than as polearms.

The koshigatana continued to be carried as a companion sword and these were mounted in the aiguchi style. An addition to the fittings in the scabbard of the koshigatana was the *kōgai*, a small blunt bodkin about 12 centimetres long which slipped into a small pocket in the side of the scabbard. Various functions have been attributed to this small skewer-like object. One is that it was used to dress the hair; another is that the rounded end was used to clean out the ears; yet another is that it was used to mark, or carry from the battlefield, the head of an enemy. Some kōgai were split, but fitted together in the scabbard by means of a small notch. These *wari-kōgai* could be used as chopsticks. Yet another addition to the mounting of the sword was the *kogatana*, a small utility knife which was also carried in a pocket in the side of the scabbard. This small knife is often erroneously referred to as a *kozuka*, a term which strictly applies only to the rectangular handle of the kogatana. The handle of the kōgai, together with the kozuka, soon became an artistic medium for the metalworkers who produced the various other metal mountings of the sword, and some were particularly lavishly decorated.

With the fall of Kamakura and the loss of their major patrons, many swordsmiths returned to their home provinces to work for the increasingly powerful regional warlords, the Shugo. These regional military governors gained considerable powers during the Nambokuchō and following Muromachi periods and many became the de-facto rulers of the provinces, some attaining the status of *daimyō*, 'great landholding name'. Some swordsmiths who are believed to have studied with Masamune in Kamakura set

23 Tachi blade signed 'Bishū Osafune Morimitsu' (Morimitsu of Osafune in Bizen), 14th century. The heavily shortened blade (perhaps by as much as 10 cm) has a strong gunome chōji-hamon (see plate 22 for the mounting). Sir Claude MacDonald, to whom this blade was given by 'Prince Katsura' (according to V&A records), was British Ambassador to Japan from 1905 to 1912 and had a particular interest in swords. The V&A was given four splendid swords by his widow, Lady Ethel MacDonald.

V&A: M.139–1929, MacDonald Gift.

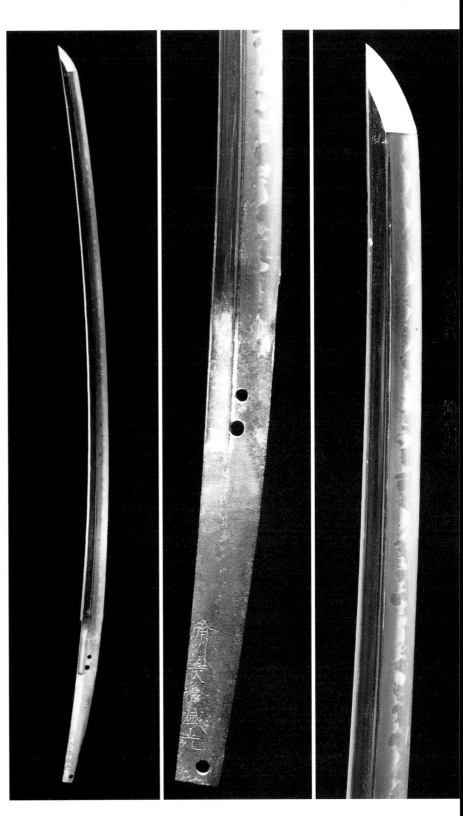

24 Naginata blade signed
'Bishū Osafune ju Kagemitsu'
(Kagemitsu, resident of Osafune
in Bizen) and 'Genkō ni nen,
hachi gatsu, hi' (a day in the
eighth month of the second year
of the Genkō period [equivalent
to 1322]). Kagemitsu of Bizen
was one of the master smiths
who produced fine, long
naginata as a direct response to
the experience of battles with
the Mongols on Japanese soil
late in the previous century.
Collection of the Tokyo National
Museum, Important Cultural Property.

25 Katana blade attributed
to Sadamune. This unsigned
14th-century blade by Sadamune
is in katakiriha-zukuri, the
omote is in shinogi-zukuri while
the ura is in hira-zukuri.
Both sides have a long hi which
on the omote extends into the
nakago. The ura also has a
carving of a *suken* and a *bonji*
(see p.25).
Collection of the Tokyo National
Museum, Important Cultural Property.

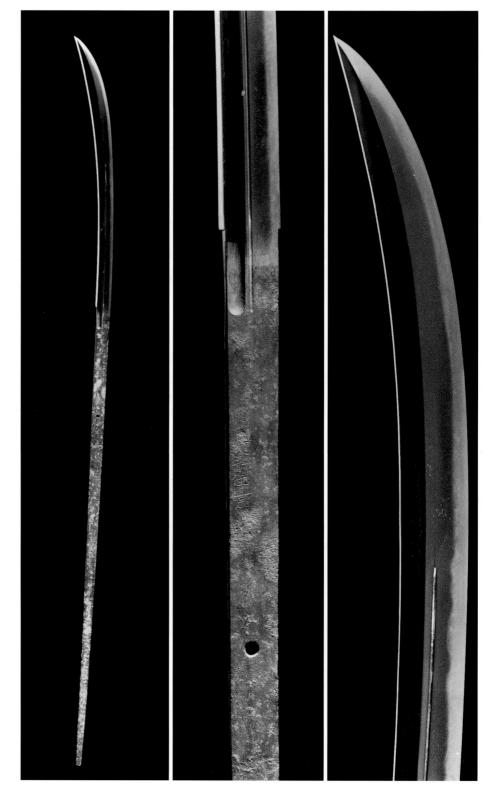

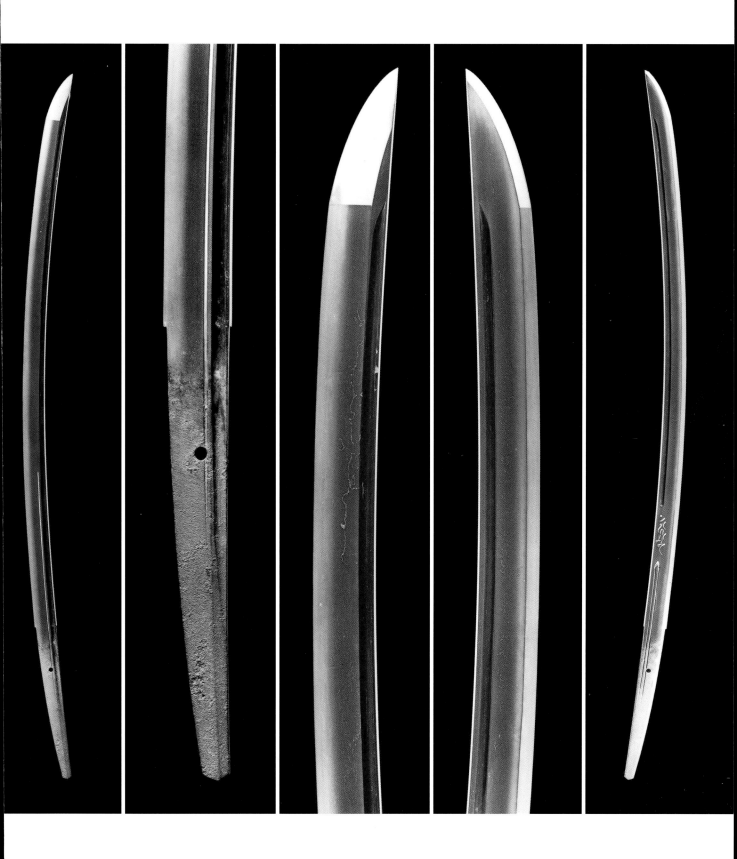

up in the provinces. These included Sadamune, who according to some sources was the son of Masamune. No signed blades by Sadamune exist today although many bear attributions (plate 25).

The swordsmith Saburō Kaneuji, who was also believed to have been one of Masamune's pupils, moved to Shizu in Mino province, where he is credited with establishing the last of the Gokaden, the Mino school, which was to flourish during the Muromachi period. Mino blades are characterized by a jihada of mixed itame and masame which is strong in jinie in the form of chikei. The hamon are ko-midare, notare or gunome and are rich in nie with lines of sunagashi. Expressive hamon became the trademark of Mino blades, particularly in later years when styles such as *sambonsugi* – 'triple cryptomeria' shape – became fashionable.

During the closing years of the Nambokuchō period Kanemitsu of the Bizen school produced many excellent large blades with hamon of gunome or notare. The Sagami school introduced a new distinctive style of hamon known as *hitatsura*. The distinguishing feature of this pattern is that the areas of tempering are not confined to a line which follows the edge of the blade, but can be found in irregular patterns over the whole blade, extending at times over the shinogi. This can at times seem rather unattractive and can give an almost 'diseased' appearance, but when executed skilfully it can result in a striking patterning on the surface of the blade.

Sengoku Jidai: the 'Period of the Warring Provinces'

The brief unification of the country under the Ashikaga shōguns presented an opportunity for the resumption of trade with China and for the cultivation of many of the refined arts of Japan. These included the codification and consolidation of the arts of the Nō theatre, which was patronized by the Ashikaga shōguns; the development of the Tea Ceremony; and the study of Zen Buddhism and its influence on the fine arts, notably *suiboku* (ink painting). Arguments over shōgunal succession within the Ashikaga family, combined with poor judgement in the application of government, led to various uprisings which eventually threw the country into turmoil. These successional quarrels resulted in the Ōnin wars, which were fought between 1467 and 1477, and were the beginnings of what was to become a century of continuous, although at times rather sporadic, civil wars, earning the period the appellation of the Sengoku Jidai, the 'Period of the Warring Provinces'.

Many of the Shugo daimyō had found themselves on opposing sides during these successional disputes and this conflict of loyalty only served to highlight their own personal factional in-fighting. The power of the Ashikaga shōguns was particularly weak and many minor provincial leaders exploited this opportunity to increase personal control over their own domains. Although the successional dispute was settled in 1473, the fighting raged in Kyoto until 1477, by which time much of the city had been devastated by fire and it seemed that the warring factions were out of control and intent on mutual destruction. Central government had all but totally collapsed and many nobles and powerful priests fled to the provinces to seek refuge or to consolidate their positions. The country was riven by inter-clan fighting on a large scale, which by now was being carried out mainly by massed armies of foot soldiers, the *ashigaru*, armed primarily with spears and swords.

The reasons behind this warring period are far from clear, and there is no single cause which can account for it. There was possibly an element of what is called in Japanese *gekokujō* – 'the low oppress the high' – a term which applies to the overthrow of the ruling classes, be they military or aristocratic, by the lower social orders. Examples of this are to be found throughout Japanese history and the term was in use at least since 1333 and the overthrow of the Kamakura Bakufu. Gekokujō as applied to the Muromachi period refers mainly to the seizure of power both locally and nationally by provincial warlords, formerly vassals of the major warrior families. In addition, there was the growing strength of independent localized warriors and small landowners known collectively as *ji-zamurai,* who banded together to form leagues (*ikki*) to resist pressures and to form local defences against other local warlords and the oppression of nationally appointed deputies. The term ikki has connotations which imply revolt and there were frequent uprisings against the Ashikaga shōguns.

The Shugo daimyō, originally appointed by central government, were slowly being replaced by the Sengoku daimyō, regional warlords who through force of arms, skilful alliances and personal strength of character gained control over the provinces. The expansion of individual territories, the constant warring and the need for larger armies produced an unusual situation whereby, despite the nationwide disruptions to government, the market for horses, arms and armour, together with that for the necessary provisioning of troops and for building materials for fortifications to local headquarters, had never been more buoyant. Many merchants and artisans in the emerging castle towns (*jōkamachi*) were required to produce supplies on an extremely large scale and as a result of this the quality of many items, notably swords and armour, suffered considerably.

The town of Seki in Mino manufactured blades on a near mass-production scale during the Muromachi period to meet the growing demand for swords for the ever-increasing numbers of samurai who were by now fighting in massed ranks on foot. Consequently there were many swords produced of little aesthetic merit, being purely practical cutting weapons and lacking any great artistic distinction. At the same time at Osafune in Bizen blades were also mass-produced and these too were pure fighting weapons of little, or no, artistic merit. These mass-produced blades were referred to as *sokutō,* 'bundled swords', or *kazu uchi mono,* 'mass-produced thing', a term which carried with it a certain note of contempt.

There was still a demand for excellent blades forged with care by smiths of the Gokaden, but the requirements for substantial numbers of swords during this period meant that there could never be enough of these fine blades produced. Consequently there were many swords forged, to which were falsely added the names of renowned smiths of the time. This can create problems with the identification of blades of this period. For example, a poor sword with a good signature could be a case of the smith trying to produce too much to satisfy demand. Likewise a good utilitarian sword of this period could be inscribed with a completely fake signature which otherwise would be its only failing.

The almost complete change in the style of warfare during the Muromachi period from battles involving cavalry and individual combat to those involving infantry with the use of regiments of foot soldiers brought about the further development and

increasing use of a different form of long sword, which had previously only been utilized by the lower ranks of foot soldier. This was the *uchigatana*, a term applied to a style
of sword which had been in use since the Kamakura period. Most of these early uchigatana, being for the common soldier, were not particularly well made and no positively identifiable examples exist today. However, during the Muromachi period
samurai of rank began to carry these blades as a supplement to the tachi and much finer
examples of this category of swords began to be produced.

The uchigatana was forged in two different sizes; those longer than approximately 60
centimetres were called *katana*, but the Muromachi period also saw the introduction of
shorter blades known as *wakizashi*, or 'companion swords'. The katana was carried
thrust through a sash with the cutting edge uppermost and was secured by a cord
(*sageo*) tied through a protrusion on the scabbard called a *kurikata* (chestnut shape). Further down the scabbard was a hooked projection called a *kaeri-tsuno*, 'return horn',
which prevented the scabbard from being pulled right out of the sash when the sword
was drawn. The practical advantage of the katana over the tachi for the foot soldier was
that the action of drawing the sword effectively became the striking blow all in one
movement. Also, being a shorter and therefore lighter blade, the katana could be more
easily used with one hand. This was of particular advantage in the intense close-combat
infantry battles, characteristic of the Muromachi period, where the speed of the draw of
the sword was of the essence. A distinctive alteration to the curvature of the blade
assisted with this continuous drawing and cutting action. The curvature of the katana,
which had moved away from the hilt to become a deep curve in the upper part of the
blade, is what is described as *saki-zori*. The saki-zori curve was also useful to the
mounted samurai as the tachi required two distinct actions of drawing and cutting.

The wakizashi were carried by the ashigaru as an additional weapon to their spears
and were far more effective in close combat than their lengthy polearms (plate 26).
When the katana and wakizashi were worn together by the samurai they were called
the *daishō*, the 'great and the small'. By the end of the Muromachi period the daishō had
became the standard wear for the samurai with the wakizashi being carried at all times
and the katana being worn when in battle or on formal occasions. Earlier uchigatana
tended to lack a tsuba, but later both swords of the daishō invariably possessed this
form of hand-guard. The blades were frequently mounted in finely lacquered or otherwise lavishly decorated scabbards, and their fittings, at least for the wealthy or high-
ranking samurai, also became increasingly luxurious.

Katana followed the custom of bearing the swordsmith's signature on the omote, the
side of the nakago away from the body. Consequently katana and tachi have signatures
on opposite sides of the blade. The position of the signature is generally an indication of
how the blade was carried, in tachi or katana style, but unfortunately there are many
exceptions to this rule. There was a long-established tradition of altering the Japanese
sword to suit personal taste or prevalent fighting conditions. A sword could be shortened to suit an individual's size or strength, or just to reflect his personal taste. During
this shortening process, which results in a blade being referred to as *suriage*, any authentic signature could be lost as the sword was always shortened at the nakago. There are
many instances of older tachi being shortened and remounted as katana and in later
periods of katana being remounted as tachi.

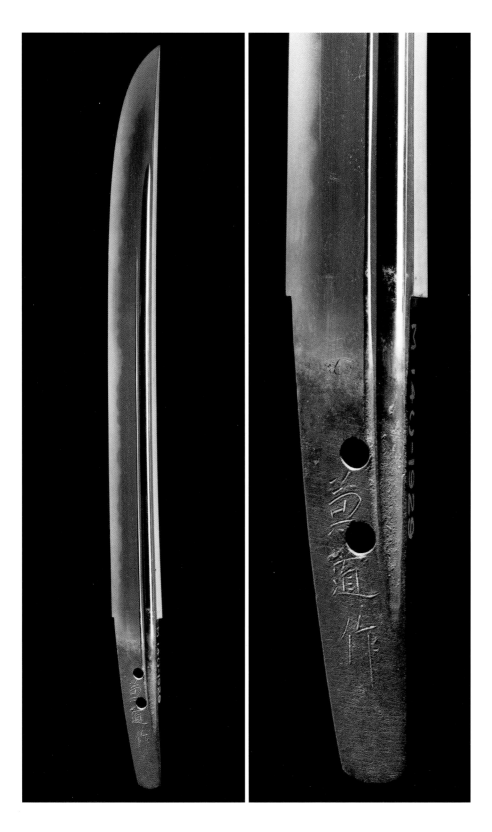

26 Wakizashi blade signed 'Kanemichi saku' (made by Kanemichi). The characteristics of this blade are typical of the simple and functional blades produced by the smiths of Seki in Mino province during the 16th century.

V&A: M.140–1929, MacDonald Gift.

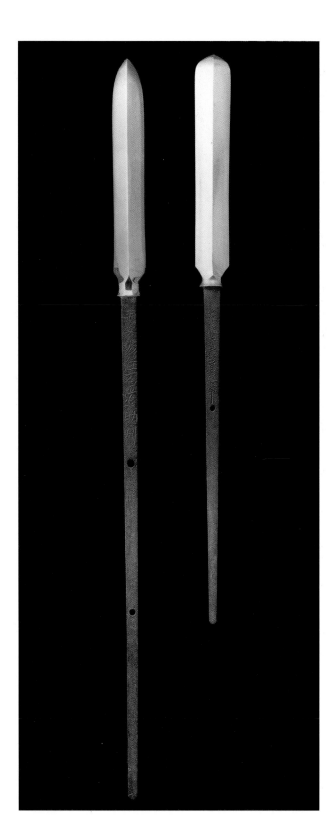

Tachi continued to be made in the Muromachi period, and these too displayed the distinctive saki-zori curve. Swords of the early Muromachi period tended to reflect the Kamakura styles with their relatively narrow blades and shorter kissaki. Some swords were less thick from the shinogi towards the mune in the style called *oroshi mune*. This type of sword was lighter in weight and had a flatter cross-section, which possibly reduced the amount of friction when cutting through armour. The general trend, however, was for swords with a more even breadth throughout their length and with slightly longer and more angular kissaki.

The saki-zori curvature of sword blades is also to be found on naginata of the period which were made somewhat shorter than the large blades of the preceding Nambokuchō period and displayed a larger curvature near the elongated point. Polearms were the main weapon of the ashigaru, and in addition to the naginata, which was primarily a cutting weapon, the use of yari became particularly widespread. The yari was used as both a slashing and a thrusting weapon, but not for throwing, and despite its length it was also employed by cavalry of the period both as a lance and for slashing cuts. There were many variants in the shape and configuration of the yari blade (which derives its form from the Nara-period *hoko*). The simple, straight, double-edged blade ranged in length from approximately 5 centimetres to over 60 centimetres, excluding the nakago. In cross-section the most common type presented a shallow triangular profile with a broad flat side backed by a shallow-ridged rear; this was called *sankaku-zukuri*, 'three cornered form'. The other most common type was a shorter, stubby blade, which presented a flattened diamond-shaped cross-section called *ryō-shinogi zukuri* (plate 27).

Unusual types of yari include the *jūmonji yari*, a central blade with two shorter horizontal spurs which resulted in a cross-shape similar to the Japanese character for the

27 Pair of yari blades: Sankaku-zukuri-yari (left), signed 'Heianjo ju Ishidō Suketoshi' (Ishidō Suketoshi resident of Heianjo – three generations from *c*.1624 to 1704 signed Suketoshi); su-yari (right), originally mounted as a nage-yari (on a short pole for close-quarters use) and signed 'Mino no Kami Fujiwara Masatsune' (Fujiwara Masatsune of Mino province), *c*.1615–24.

V&A: M.95–1919, Dobrée Gift; 703–1908, Davison Gift.

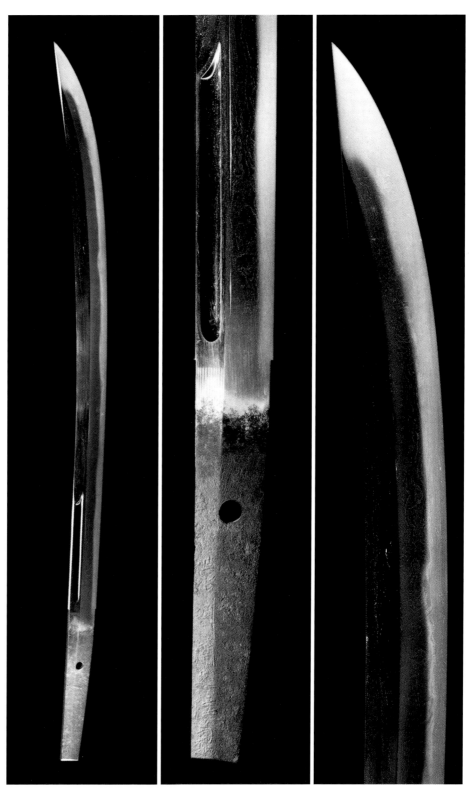

28 Wakizashi blade in kammuri-otoshi style, signed 'Noshū Seki no Ju Kane…' (Kane…, resident of Seki in Noshū [Mino]), tang suriage, 16th century. The blade clearly shows strong masame and mokume graining with lines of nioi along the gently undulating hamon, and has been shortened with the loss of the final character of the smith's signature. It may even have been converted from a naginata blade into a wakizashi.

V&A: anonymous loan.

number ten, *jū*. The *katakama yari* has a vertical blade with a single horizontal spur of almost equivalent length, which is frequently slightly curved and sometimes possesses a second short protrusion following the line of the horizontal blade. There were many other fanciful configurations of yari blades, some of more ceremonial than purely effective practical use. Many yari blades of the sankaku-zukuri form had a central groove (*hi*) running from the nakago almost to the point, which lightened the blade somewhat. Sometimes this hi is filled with red lacquer, although this practice was possibly carried out as a later addition to the blade. The more rudimentary and purely functional spears were rarely signed, but some notable swordsmiths from the Gokaden produced signed yari.

Various forms of daggers continued to be made in considerable numbers throughout the Muromachi period, all reflecting the continuing trend towards close-combat fighting and the need for shorter personal weapons in those situations. Many of these daggers, like the swords of this period, hark back to the earlier Kamakura styles. A special type of dagger called a *yoroi-doshi* (armour-piercer) was produced in great numbers, although this form of tantō is known to have been in existence since the Kamakura period. The yoroi-doshi is a short, thick triangular sectioned blade, ideally suited to penetrating lamellar armour at close quarters. Other daggers in the slightly curved and double-edged *moroha-zukuri* configuration were being made by the Bizen and Mino schools. Tantō in u-no-kubi and kammuri-otoshi styles, previously associated only with the Yamato schools of the Kamakura period, were also now being made by many other schools (plate 28).

Although the Muromachi period is characterized by the mass production of swords, there were still many smiths of the Gokaden producing fine blades and introducing interesting and distinctive variations in the hamon patterns of the blade. At Seki in Mino the traditions established by Kaneuji were continued by a number of smiths who all signed their names beginning with the character *Kane* taken from the name of the founder of the school. Kanemoto developed the distinctive style of hamon called sambonsugi, a variation on the spiky hamon of Kaneuji. There were three early Muromachi smiths using the name Kanemoto, and the second, Magoroku Kanemoto, was renowned for the cutting ability of his blades (plate 29).

Kanefusa developed an especially undulating form of gunome hamon, which had rounded peaks and became known as 'priest's head' gunome, and another form called *fukuro gunome chōji*, 'pouch' chōji. The cutting ability of Kanefusa's swords was clearly shown in the Edo period when one especially broad-bladed sword was allegedly used to cut through seven bodies in a test of the blade, although this form of test also illustrated the ability of the person using the sword. The smith Kanesada was notable for hamon of strong gunome chōji of angular form known as *uma no ha gunome*, 'horse's teeth gunome' (plate 30).

In Bizen, the other major centre of mass production of swords, smiths such as Yasumitsu and Morimitsu produced blades which followed the older traditions of the school and had suguha hamon with accompanying utsuri or were of strong gunome chōji. Utsuri tended to disappear from Bizen blades in the later Muromachi period and distinctive forms of nie in the blade became the major characteristic. One particularly fanciful hamon was created by Sukesada, a name which came to be used by literally

29 Wakizashi blade signed 'Kanemoto' (of Seki), *c.*1530. The blade has a strong sambon sugi hamon. On the omote side of the blade is carved a later horimono of the bodhisattva Monju standing on a *shishi* (mythical lion-dog); the ura of the blade bears the bonji for Fudo and a stylized *rendai* (Buddhist lotus throne). V&A: M.28-1912.

30 Tantō blade signed 'Kanefusa'. The dagger features the characteristic strong gunome chōji of Kanefusa (late 16th century). The second character of the signature is, however, unclear and this, together with some other characteristics, including the relative thinness of the blade, casts some possible doubt on the authenticity of this attribution.

V&A: FE.3–1974, Crawshay Gift.

31 Wakizashi blade signed 'Bizen Kuni ju Osafune Shichibei-jo Sukesada' (Osafune Shichibeijo Sukesada resident of Bizen province) and 'Kambun roku nen hachi gatsu kichi jitsu' (a lucky day in the eighth month of the sixth year of Kambun [equivalent to 1666]). The blade clearly displays the distinctive style of hamon called kani no tsume, 'crab's claws', a form of gunome hamon with split peaks.

V&A: M.12–1947, Jahn Bequest.

dozens of later smiths. This hamon was called *kani no tsume*, 'crab's claws', and was a form of gunome hamon with split peaks (plate 31). The hitatsura hamon previously associated with the Sagami school was increasingly to be found on the blades of the Mino and Bizen schools as the Muromachi period progressed.

The swords of one notable Muromachi-period smith, Muramasa of Ise, have gained a particularly notorious reputation. His swords display many of the characteristics of the Mino and Sagami schools and have varying forms of hamon including strong gunome,

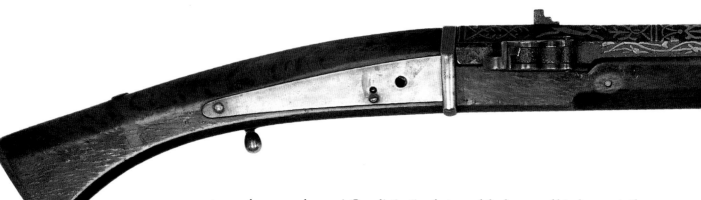

notare and even sambonsugi. One distinctive feature of the hamon of his daggers is the deepness of their 'troughs', which can at times come almost to the edge of the blade. There were believed to have been three smiths using this name, and all of their blades are reputed to cut well. However, Muramasa blades have acquired a distinctly sinister status in Japan as they allegedly caused death or injury to members of the Tokugawa family, the ruling shōguns during the Edo period. Various prohibitions were imposed by the Tokugawa shōguns regarding the carrying of Muramasa's swords.

They were extremely effective weapons, and as a result of these prohibitions blades bearing this signature were often altered by removing the character *Mura* and adding the character *Mune* after *Masa*, thereby changing the name to *Masamune*, the greatest of all Japanese swordsmiths. This practice may have led to the confusion and widely held belief that Muramasa was the pupil of Masamune, but Muramasa was in fact making swords some two hundred years after the time of Masamune. Several stories have evolved regarding the inherent properties of Muramasa's blades. One of the most evocative and poetic describes an occasion when two swords were hung from a bridge into the gently flowing water below. One sword was by Masamune, the other by Muramasa. As the autumn leaves floated by in the stream they drifted away from Masamune's sword but were drawn irresistibly towards Muramasa's blade and were cut in half.

By the mid-sixteenth century Japan was a divided country with no effective national ruler, the emperor being isolated in Kyoto where the ineffectual Ashikaga Bakufu were also attempting to exert their authority. The countryside was controlled by various regional daimyō and minor warlords who formed alliances, and broke them as quickly, as and when the occasion suited. It seems fateful, then, that in 1543 the shipwreck of a Portuguese trading vessel (or, according to other more likely accounts, a Chinese vessel with three Portuguese on board) on the island of Tanegashima off the southern coast of

Kyūshū was soon to bring about yet another major change in warfare in Japan. In the cargo of the ship were a number of matchlock muskets, and the effectiveness of this new weapon was such that they were soon being copied in considerable quantities by Japanese metalworkers, especially by swordsmiths who quickly adapted their sword-making technology to producing guns (plate 32).

Up until this moment Japan had been trading almost exclusively with China and this was the first real point of contact with Europe and its newer forms of technology and

religious ideas, both of which were to have a profound influence on events in Japan over the following hundred years. This period has become known as Japan's Christian Century. The Portuguese, who had been trading out of China, soon departed and took word of Japan with them. Within a few years they had returned to the ports of Kyūshū with trade goods and missionaries. The Kyūshū daimyō were eager for trade as they saw this opportunity as a means to consolidate and perhaps expand their own military strength in the warring country.

Guns were immediately recognized as a potentially important addition to the existing arsenals of the Sengoku daimyō. The ruling warlord of Tanegashima is reported to have paid an enormous amount in gold for two of the original guns, but within a year his own smiths were producing effective copies of these weapons at a relatively cheap cost. There were still several technical problems to be overcome, in particular the closing of the end of the barrel, but the original investment assuredly paid off handsomely. Within ten years specialist gunsmiths were established and producing matchlocks throughout much of Japan. They were increasingly taking over production from those swordsmiths who had previously been required to manufacture these new weapons.

The Japanese gunsmiths made many improvements to the European matchlocks, notably in the firing mechanisms, and also devised protective covers to ensure that they could be fired even in wet weather. These matchlock guns were originally called *Tanegashima* after their place of introduction, but were soon referred to as *teppō*, iron tubes or *hinawaju*. Increasingly the ashigaru, many of whom were of low samurai stock, were being trained in the use of the gun, and most armies of the late Muromachi period had significant numbers of musketeers, some in specially dedicated regiments.

A samurai would need years of training to become proficient with the bow and the sword. Likewise the yari and naginata, when used by individual warriors, were precision

32 Short matchlock gun (lacking firing mechanism) with a steel barrel inlaid in silver and brass with Christian symbols, *c.*1600–1640. This short, carbine-like matchlock was probably intended for use on horseback. The upper part of the barrel bears inlaid symbols of Christ's Passion and the weapon must have belonged to one of Japan's Christian daimyō of the early 17th century.
V&A: M.30–1937, Gardiner Gift.

weapons. When these polearms were used by the massed ranks of foot-soldiers, the
techniques were different to those for one-to-one combat. However, it needed little
training for a low-ranking samurai, or even a conscripted farmer, to become proficient
in the use of the matchlock, especially when they were fired in volleys by lines of musketeers. For this reason, while the gun was seen as a devastatingly efficient weapon, it
was never deemed an 'honourable' one, as the lowliest individual could kill, at quite
some distance, the noblest and bravest of warriors. The use of the gun by
the 'lower orders' was the death-blow to the ancient custom of declaring one's lineage
and also to the traditional charge of cavalry prior to the advance of the regiments of
foot-soldiers. Cavalry were primarily high-ranking samurai and it would have been
foolish in the extreme to have sacrificed oneself to a peasant armed with a gun.

The Momoyama period

Among the warlords of the late sixteenth century one man came to prominence. This
was Oda Nobunaga, son of a Sengoku daimyō of Owari province, and referred to as
one of the 'Three Great Unifiers of Japan'. Nobunaga inherited his father's land and
titles when aged only seventeen and he quickly established a reputation for ruthless-
ness. He seized many nearby domains through force of arms and had his own brother
killed on suspicion of plotting against him. In 1568 he was sufficiently powerful to take
Kyoto and install Ashikaga Yoshiaki as his appointed shōgun in the area of Kyoto called
Momoyama, from which this period of the later sixteenth century is known. In reality
Nobunaga controlled the shōgunate, and his private aspirations, never brought to
fruition, were evident from the words on his personal seal of this period: *Tenka Fubu*,
'The Realm under the Military'.

The devastating use of guns was clearly demonstrated at the Battle of Nagashino
when in 1575 Nobunaga defeated his long-standing enemy Takeda Katsuyori mainly
through his decisive use of approximately 3,000 matchlocks firing successively in three
ranks. Takeda's army prefaced the battle with the traditional cavalry charge and were
decimated. The common foot-soldier armed with a gun was triumphant. Honour, tradition and the martial abilities of the individual warrior, together with his prized swords
and fine armour counted for little in the face of the gun. Traditional Japanese armour
was virtually useless against the gun (at a reasonably close range) so heavy plate
armour was adopted which, while effective against the gun, slowed down the samurai
in battle when pitted against the sword. Somewhat ironically the best guns of the
period were being produced at Negoro and Saiga by the Ikkō, the heavily armed
militant Buddhist monks of the Jōdo Shin sect whom Nobunaga eventually had to
brutally crush.

An important change in the social organization during the Muromachi period was
brought about through the increasing development of the large, heavily fortified castles
of the Sengoku daimyō, around which had grown up the jōkamachi, the castle towns.
These imposing structures represented not only the power of the daimyō over his
domain, but in a period which saw almost constant warfare provided a major
defensive outpost against rivals, who were by now increasingly armed with cannon
(plate 33). The castle towns which gradually followed the building of the castles became
in time the regional administrative and commercial headquarters of the daimyō. This

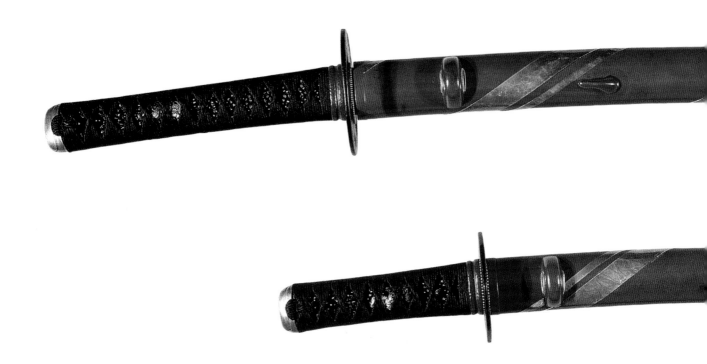

34 Sword mountings of a katana and wakizashi as a daishō in wooden scabbards decorated with red lacquer and applied spiral helical bands of gold leaf. The metal fittings are of gold with the tsuba of shakudō. The ray-skin grip of the hilt has been lacquered black before being bound in black silk over a gold menuki. The opulence of the Momoyama period is well reflected in the restrained yet sumptuous mountings of this daishō.

Collection of the Tokyo National Museum, Important Cultural Property.

development was to be a significant break in tradition, and important vassals were required to live within the boundaries of the lord's castle rather than away on their own estates where they could potentially plot and intrigue.

The jōkamachi served as regional centres of manufacture and culture, meeting the demands of the military who were yet again developing into a form of military aristocracy. As with the establishment of Yoritomo's Bakufu at Kamakura, so the craftsmen and makers of arms and armour settled in the jōkamachi under the protection and patronage of the local warlords. The traditional centres of mass sword manufacture at Osafune in Bizen and Seki in Mino were unable to sustain huge numbers of smiths, so many found their way to the regional jōkamachi, thereby dispersing the skills of these traditions of sword making to other regions of Japan.

Nobunaga was a particularly enthusiastic patron of the arts, and his castle at Azuchi overlooking Lake Biwa was decorated by famous painters of the Kanō school. The castle was described by the Portuguese Jesuit missionary and chronicler of Japan, Luis Frois, as follows:

> Nobunaga's castle, which as regards architecture, strength, wealth and grandeur may well be compared with the greatest buildings of Europe… inside, the walls are decorated with designs richly painted in gold and different colours while the outside of each storey is painted in various colours … In a word, the whole edifice is beautiful, excellent and brilliant.[3]

Nobunaga was a notably fine example of a samurai who combined ruthless efficiency on the battlefield and in politics with the sensibilities and refinements of the arts and

culture of his time. His splendid castle was, unfortunately, destroyed soon after his death in 1582.

Despite the adoption of different forms of weaponry such as polearms and guns, the sword was still by far the most treasured possession of the samurai and the preferred weapon to demonstrate ability in battle. Higher-ranking samurai still desired excellent swords, but unfortunately many of the techniques for producing such fine weapons as those from the early Muromachi period or from the Kamakura and Heian periods had been lost during the rise in demand for mass-produced blades. The tradition of shortening older swords to be remounted as katana increased, as the fashion for daishō became more prevalent. During the Momoyama period the custom for daishō to be decorated as a fully matched pair became well established (plate 34). Often the various metal fittings of the sword would also be decorated as a matching set and given a regular theme or pattern by metalworkers of the growing numbers of individual schools who specialized in this miniature art form.

The older and considerably longer tachi, designed for fighting from horseback, had been forged with their curvature near the hilt. This configuration of the blade was unsuitable for the continuous drawing and striking action required of the katana by the samurai fighting on foot. Consequently many more of the fine old swords were shortened at the hilt resulting in swords which now featured a curvature nearer the tip. During this process any original signatures were of course lost, but attributions or other forms of appraisal might well be added to the new nakago by a sword appraiser. The shortening and appraisal of blades will be dealt with in more detail later in the book.

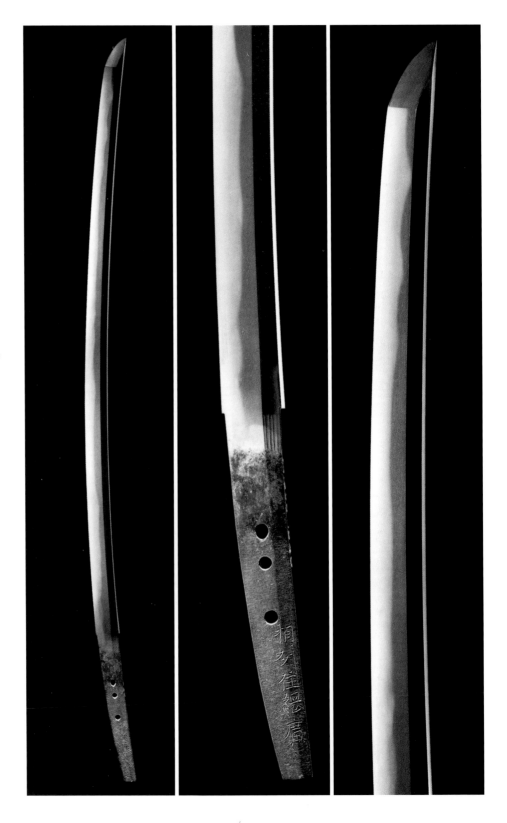

35 Katana blade signed 'Soshū ju Tsunahiro' (Tsunahiro of Soshū), late 16th century. This shortened blade is most probably the work of Tsunahiro III, who worked in Sagami province from about 1590 to 1615. The blade displays the broad, slightly notare hamon of the Soshū school, which in places extends almost as far as the shinogi. Originally the blade would have had a more even curve (see plate 54 for the shirasaya and inscription.)
V&A: M.356–1940, Gift of Colonel John C. Somerville, C.M.G., C.B.E.

The qualities of the older swords were much appreciated and smiths of the Momoyama period began to make blades which copied the shape of the earlier swords in their cut-down condition. This resulted in a sword which was broad yet thin, of an even width and with an even curve throughout the length of the blade or slightly emphasized near the tip. The ability to recreate the more aesthetic qualities found on the older blades, such as the delicate and restrained hamon with exquisite nie and nioi crystals, was by now for the most part lost. Momoyama-period swordsmiths in the provinces tended to follow the traditions of their original schools, but some newer styles began to develop (plate 35). Despite the still bitter fighting, the Momoyama period was renowned as an age of luxury and opulence. Comparisons can be made with the flourishing of culture alongside the power of the military during the establishment of the governments of Minamoto Yoritomo at Kamakura and Ashikaga Takauji at Muromachi.

Of particular note among the Momoyama-period swordsmiths was Umetada Myōju who worked in the Nishijin area of Kyoto, signing his work 'Myōju of Nishijin in Yamashiro'. Myōju was an accomplished master metalworker who, in addition to forging blades, was a maker of decorative sword fittings in soft metals. He was also considered competent enough to shorten older swords and was frequently commissioned to carry out this work and have the blades remounted as katana in daishō. Myōju's sword fittings, specifically the tsuba, were often made of different metals which were patinated or inlaid to give a finely polychromatic effect perfectly suited to the Momoyama taste. He produced mostly daggers in hira-zukuri form with itame jihada and broad notare or gunome hamon which are strong in nie. His blades frequently have exquisitely carved horimono contained within short grooves, and a common subject depicted is that of Fudō Myō-Ō together with his bonji and on the opposite side of the blade a dragon, sometimes represented wrapped around Fudō's ken sword (plate 36).

One authenticated katana signed by Myōju does exist, but there are many others with fake inscriptions, some of which are completely at variance with the style of blade normally associated with Myōju. One wonders therefore when and why these blades were made and who they were intended for. Myōju's blades were extremely desirable objects and while Japanese artistic traditions do allow for objects to be made in the style of a great master, outright fakery for profit certainly cannot be excluded.

Despite his dominance of much of the country Nobunaga did not remain unchallenged, and he continued to struggle to gain control of many of the regional daimyō, in particular the powerful Shingen family of eastern Japan. The alliance of Nobunaga and Tokugawa Ieyasu was defeated by Takeda Shingen early in 1573, causing the Shōgun Yoshiaki, previously appointed by Nobunaga, to side with Shingen in the conflict. In May 1573 Nobunaga surrounded Kyoto putting it to the torch until Yoshiaki finally surrendered and went into exile. The Muromachi shōgunate existed in name only until 1588 when Yoshiaki abdicated, Nobunaga then being the shōgun in all but name. The official title of shōgun was by tradition reserved for those who could claim direct descent from the Minamoto family. To the end of his life Nobunaga sought to unify the warring daimyō, but he was attacked by one of his retainers, Akechi Mitsuhide, in 1582 at Honnōji, a Buddhist temple in Kyoto. Fighting until severely wounded, Nobunaga finally committed *seppuku*, ritual suicide, in the burning temple rather than be taken alive by the enemy.

36 Tantō blade signed on the omote 'Yamashiro [no] Kuni Nishijin [no] Ju-nin Umetada Myōju, Keichō ju-san nen, hachi gatsu, kichi jitsu' (Umetada Myōju, resident of Nishijin in Yamashiro province, a lucky day in the thirteenth year of Keichō [equivalent to 1598]). The ura bears the inscription 'Shoji Shinzō jūdai' (in the possession of Shinzō for successive generations). This is a superb example of a genuine blade by Umetada Myōju and the hira-zukuri tantō displays most of the characteristics to be found in his work. The blade has a bright itame ground and a broad hamon with gentle undulations. The horimono of the descending dragon chasing the hōkyū (Buddhist Treasure Jewel) and that of Fudō Myō-Ō and his bonji are equally fine examples of Myōju's carved work.
Private Collection.

Almost immediately, Toyotomi Hideyoshi, one of Nobunaga's generals who had risen through the ranks from his humble beginnings as the son of a low-ranking ashigaru, seized power by the usual manner of skilful alliances and successful battles. In time-honoured tradition he redistributed strategic fiefs to trustworthy allies, thus drastically reducing the powers of the provincial daimyō. By 1585 he had assumed all civil and military power in the name of the emperor and was appointed *kampaku*, or regent. At the time of his death Nobunaga had secured control over more than a third of the country and Hideyoshi continued to push these conquests over rival daimyō. Firstly he secured positions to the west, particularly against the Shimizu family of Satsuma in Kyūshū. In 1587 he sent an immense army, said to number some 200,000, against Shimizu. Hideyoshi's troops carried guns as well as traditional weapons whereas the Satsuma armies, not for the last time in history, were armed only with traditional weaponry. Within a relatively short period the Satsuma armies were defeated, but Hideyoshi resolved not to massacre his opponents, unlike Nobunaga may have done, settling rather on a diplomatic solution and appointing his own trusted commanders to oversee parts of Kyūshū, leaving the Shimizu family with some control.

The last major barriers to Hideyoshi's attempts to unify Japan were overcome in 1590 at the long battle of Odawara when the Hōjō family, long-time rulers of the Kantō, were finally defeated, and the following year saw the crushing of smaller pockets of resistance in the far north of Japan. All Japanese territories were now ruled either directly by Hideyoshi or by his trusted vassals. With the unification of Japan complete, Hideyoshi then began a series of disastrous grandiose campaigns against Korea, with the ultimate aim of conquering China. The Japanese armies withdrew from the first campaign against Korea in 1592 after encountering strong resistance from both the Koreans, who fought with guerrilla tactics, and the forces of Ming China, although pockets of Japanese forces maintained small bases in parts of southern Korea. Political discussions between Japan, Korea and China continued for several years until in 1597 a new attack, aimed directly at China, was launched through Korea. The wars continued through 1598 until Japanese troops, who had fought valiantly against overwhelming odds in difficult circumstances, were finally evacuated following Hideyoshi's death.

Hideyoshi had earlier instigated further forms of regional control through various expedient policies, such as his famous sword-hunt in 1588, the *katanagari*, whereby all non-samurai were deprived of weapons. Through this, the likelihood of armed rebellion was greatly reduced and the separation of the samurai class from the peasantry was further increased. The centres of the samurai power structure now lay fully in the castle towns rather than in the agricultural world where the samurai had traditionally had their roots. One professed reason for the katanagari was to provide iron nails and bolts to build a huge wooden figure of Buddha for the new monastery of Hōkōji which Hideyoshi was to establish in Kyoto. Hideyoshi's edict stipulated that:

> The people of the various provinces are strictly forbidden to have in their possession any swords, short swords, bows, spears, firearms or any other types of arms... Swords and short swords collected in this way will not be wasted and they will be melted down and used in the construction of the Great Image of the Buddha.

The peasants were told that by thus contributing to the Buddha image they would be assured of salvation both in this life and in the next.

Finally, through the population census of 1590 which bound the peasants even further to the land and their local lords, Hideyoshi formalized the four social classes which were to be the mainstay of Japan for the next 300 years. These class distinctions were, in order of their importance, the samurai (*shi*), farmers (*nō*), artisans (*kō*) and merchants (*shō*), this grouping being collectively known as the *shi-nō-kō-shō*. The emperor and imperial family were nominally above this hierarchy, but in reality were completely under the control of the military. Through both the katanagari and the population census large numbers of provincial samurai were effectively disenfranchised and many masterless samurai were thrown out into the countryside. These were called *rōnin*, 'wave men', and they had to try and find a new lord to serve or some other meaningful form of employment, although many found less socially acceptable means of maintaining a living. Many rōnin had also been created through Hideyoshi's defeat of provincial daimyō, and this group of leaderless warriors were to feature prominently in Japanese society for a considerable time hereafter.

Among those swordsmiths who studied with Umetada Myōju was Horikawa Kunihiro. Kunihiro was an exceptionally interesting character who came from Hyūgen in Kyūshū where he was a retainer of the Itō family. Following Hideyoshi's attacks on the warlords of Kyūshū in 1587, Kunihiro became a rōnin and wandered Japan practising his sword making wherever he could. From some time around 1596 he settled in Ichijō Horikawa in Kyoto, establishing his own distinctive school of swordsmiths, and himself trained many distinguished pupils. Blades produced from this time, the beginning of the Keichō era, are designated as *shintō*, 'new swords', and Kunihiro is often referred to as 'the father of shintō'. His blades are noted for their bright jinie jihada and full notare, midare or gunome hamon which have abundant nie and at times reach almost to the shinogi. Kunihiro based much of his work on the early Sagami styles of sword making, and his broad swords with even curvature and large kissaki greatly resemble a cut-down early blade.

Tadayoshi of Hizen, also from the island of Kyūshū, was adopted by a swordsmith when he was orphaned. Some time around 1596, when aged about twenty-four, he went to Kyoto and spent two years studying under Umetada Myōju. He was then appointed as official swordsmith to the ruling family of Nabeshima in their castle town of Saga back in his home province of Hizen. He took back with him some of the characteristics of the blades of his master Myōju, combining the bright itame hada and nie notare hamon with the Hizen traditions of ko-itame hada and evenly distributed ji-nie, which were called *ko-nuka hada*, 'rice-flour hada', an extremely fine form of nie. Like Myōju, the swords of Tadayoshi often featured fine horimono of dragons carved along the shinogi. These are delicately carved and have long slender necks and bodies, often entwined around a ken. Several generations of smiths signed using the name Tadayoshi and their elegant restrained suguha hamon are reminiscent of the work of the fourteenth-century smith Rai Kunimitsu of Yamashiro. Their work also featured gunome midare and chōji hamon.

The wakizashi, adopted as the smaller of the two swords of the daishō, has in some ways a similar relationship to the katana as the tantō has to the tachi. It has been suggested that the wakizashi was a weapon better suited to closer forms of fighting or for use in confined spaces such as in narrow streets or indoors (plate 37). The wakizashi was certainly carried at all times and provision was made for the samurai to leave his katana on a special rack (*katana-kake*) when entering a house or an audience room. This served the immediate purpose of disarming him of his long sword and additionally showing his peaceful intentions, although the long sword would in any case be difficult to wield indoors. The long sword was the symbol of the samurai's authority and his honour, so this temporary setting aside of the blade was an act loaded with symbolism. However, he would be allowed to carry in his wakizashi, but unless he was an absolutely and completely trusted individual, he would be required to remove even this weapon, placing it on the floor with the handle towards the host.

In the latter part of the sixteenth century the tantō generally fell into disuse as a weapon for battles and tended to be carried at all times by older samurai or worn by higher-ranking samurai when at home. The older and longer tantō, many of which were fine blades, were frequently remounted as wakizashi and worn as part of the daishō. There had always been even smaller forms of dagger which could be secreted about the person, frequently hidden within the long dangling sleeves of the kimono, and these weapons could be used to deadly effect for assassination purposes. Samurai women in particular carried a small dagger known as a *kaiken*. This could be used as an offensive weapon or to commit suicide in extreme situations by severing the jugular vein and thereby avoiding dishonour. This form of suicide was unique to women, but other forms of ritual suicide will be discussed later in the book.

On the death of Hideyoshi in 1598 yet another power struggle broke out among the remaining powerful daimyō over the succession to the national hegemony, and Japan was again plunged into civil strife. The most powerful of these daimyō was Tokugawa Ieyasu who, as one of the 'Five Great Elders', had pledged allegiance to Hideyoshi's nominated successor Hideyori shortly before Hideyoshi's death. Following the Battle of Odawara in 1590 Ieyasu had accepted Hideyoshi's offer (not lightly refused) of the new fief of the Kantō in eastern Japan, based at the then small town of Edo. This required him giving up his native provinces around Mikawa and moving his family and vassals to a new and completely unfamiliar province. However, Edo quickly grew and in a short time had become a major castle town under Ieyasu. The country was now broadly divided between the eastern daimyō loyal to Ieyasu and the western daimyō under Ishida Mitsunari, loyal to Hideyori. By forming new alliances and encouraging hostages to be sent to him (a long established practice – Ieyasu himself had been a hostage in his youth), Ieyasu broke many of his promises to Hideyoshi.

In 1600 the western supporters of Hideyori clashed with the eastern forces of Ieyasu at the Battle of Sekigahara. The battle was decisively won only after the late defection during the battle itself by five of the western daimyō to Ieyasu's side. The outcome of this struggle was the assumption by Ieyasu of most of Hideyoshi's powers and the control of Kyoto (and therefore the emperor). On the strength of tenuous links showing Minamoto descendance, Ieyasu was proclaimed shōgun in 1603 by Emperor Go-Yozei. Despite victory at Sekigahara, Ieyasu was still dependent on the support of other daimyō. Any discontent with the Tokugawa shōgunate could result in daimyō rallying around Hideyori and bringing down Ieyasu. Fiefdoms were confiscated from those who had fought against Ieyasu at Sekigahara and given to those who had supported him.

Ieyasu eventually realized that the only way to control the country totally was to wipe out the last trace of the Toyotomi family, and so in the winter of 1614 and once again in the spring of 1615 Ieyasu stormed Osaka Castle, the last stronghold of Hideyori. Many of those daimyō formerly loyal to Hideyori were by that time either dead or in no position to provide assistance. Thousands of rōnin, many of whom had been dispossessed by Ieyasu's redistribution of fiefdoms, swarmed to Osaka and rallied around Hideyori in what appeared to them to be a last chance of finding honourable service for their swords and to avenge their former masters on Ieyasu. The vast numbers of Ieyasu's forces prevailed and Hideyori committed suicide rather than be taken. He was no longer able to put any trust in the word of Ieyasu who, even during the assault on Osaka Castle, had promised his safety. Hideyori's seven-year-old son Kunimatsu was later beheaded. In his rise to power Ieyasu had repeatedly broken his promises, but Japan was at last truly united under the Tokugawa family whose shōgunate was to last until 1867.

37 Wakizashi signed 'Mishina [or Sanpin] Izumi Fujiwara Rai Kinmichi [or Kanemichi]' (Fujiwara Rai Kinmichi, Mishina in Izumi province) and 'Nihon Kaji sosho [+ Kiku mon]' (Master Smith of Japan [+ chrysanthemum crest]). The style of the signature on the tang is extremely graceful, but tends to lack some of the strength of that of the first-generation 'Sanpin' Rai Kinmichi. There were four recognized smiths who signed in this style but the third-generation Kinmichi, who used precisely this form of signature, worked during the Empō period (1673–81).
The inscription on the ura appears to have been added later by a different hand and confusingly the later smiths of this group used the term 'Master Smith of Japan'.
V&A: 651–1908, Davison Gift.

5 | The Edo Period 1600–1868

The sword and the samurai in peacetime

Tokugawa Ieyasu recognized that many of the provincial daimyō could still present problems and through a series of extremely careful moves established family, relatives and vassals, together with those who pledged loyalty to the new shōgunate, in various positions of authority. These loyal supporters were known as the *Fudai daimyō* and included those who had backed Ieyasu at the Battle of Sekigahara. Those powerful daimyō who had either remained neutral at Sekigahara or had offered their allegiance after the battle were termed *Tozama daimyō*, 'Outside lords'. They were treated with a circumspect regard by Ieyasu but had their provinces constantly watched by the extensive network of Bakufu spies as well as having an enforced physical separation from each other through the appointment of Fudai daimyō in adjacent territories, which further reduced the possibility of planned uprisings.

The Tozama were also the first to be called upon to provide corvée labour and building materials for the repair of strategic castles for Ieyasu, thus proving their 'loyalty' and at the same time being deprived of their income and having their vassals effectively employed on behalf of Ieyasu. The Fudai daimyō had their own difficulties in that they were sometimes moved into different provinces by the shōgunate for purely political reasons, which meant that they were then often unable to establish a reliable infrastructure in these temporarily allocated provinces.

In 1615 Ieyasu laid down a series of rules of behaviour for the military classes; these were the *Buke Sho-Hatto*, 'Laws of the Military Houses'. Even from before the establishment of the Kamakura Bakufu there had been some form of codification of the laws relating to the warrior houses. These were known as the *Bukehō*, a series of regulations which governed the behaviour of warriors and, increasingly, their vassals. Ieyasu took these ancient laws even further and included rules of behaviour not only for the military but for the imperial household, aristocrats (*kuge*), Shintō shrines and Buddhist temples. The Tokugawa Bakufu enlisted a notable group of Confucian and Zen scholars to help with the preparation of these codes of behaviour.

The principal articles of these laws required the samurai to study both military arts and civil learning and to be of sober demeanour in their daily life and in their actions, thereby setting an example to all the other classes. Social relationships were clearly defined and the laws attempted to ensure that everyone knew their place in society and, what is more important, that they kept to that place and did not disturb the status quo. These rules remained in force in one form or another, with various adjustments from time to time, until the fall of the Tokugawa Shōgunate in 1867.

Above all, the Buke Sho-Hatto required that the samurai maintain their military standing even in times of peace, and the very first of the regulations stipulated: 'The study of literature and the practice of the military arts must be pursued side by side.' The regulations went further in restricting movement out of the home fiefdom, yet at the same time required that wrongdoers should be expelled, an approach which was to contribute further to the increasing problem of the numbers of the rōnin. Ieyasu's own words sum up succinctly the importance of military training and the developing dual nature of the samurai:

> The Way of letters and of arms, of archery and of horsemanship must be cultivated with all the heart and mind. In times of order we cannot forget disorder; how then can we relax our military training? The sword is the soul of the warrior. If any forget or lose it he will not be excused. (Plate 38)

The feeling of insecurity within the shōgunate regarding possible insurrection was reflected in the issuing of many further legal codes and proscriptions regarding ways of behaviour, dress and the size of swords and who could carry them. Other methods of shōgunal control were the police system of spies, inspectors and formal censors employed by the shōgunate in the provinces. There was also the National Seclusion Policy (*Sakoku*) created between 1633 and 1639, which prohibited Japanese from leaving the country (and prevented those already abroad from returning) and restricted foreign trade to specific controlled areas of the country. The proselytising Spanish and Portuguese Catholics were excluded, but the Protestant Dutch continued to trade.

Christianity had by this time been prohibited, since it was seen by the shōgunate as subversive and potentially presenting similar problems to those of the earlier militant Buddhist sects. Total loyalty was demanded by the shōgunate who regarded the allegiance to a foreign god as undermining their own authority. Some daimyō had adopted Christianity and their vassals naturally followed, creating particular problems of loyalty. In addition to ending the potential threat of Christianity, Sakoku sought to avoid any possible foreign interference in the shōgunate's aim of establishing lasting internal peace and prosperity within Japan.

39 Daishō mounting. The subtle and restrained mountings of this katana and wakizashi are characterized by matt black lacquer scabbards which are decorated in low relief with stylized clouds in a slightly glossier black lacquer. The metal fittings are mostly of shakudō with details in gold although there are some shibuichi fittings. Many are signed by well-known makers of the late 17th and early 19th centuries and include members of the Gotō school. The daishō was probably assembled around 1840.

V&A: M.20 & 21–1949, Alt Bequest.

The sumptuary laws required that Samurai in service adopt a particular form of hair-style, where the front of the head was shaven and the hair at the back pulled back into a queue in the style known as *chommage*. There was also a standard form of dress in Edo known as the *kamishimo*. This comprised a matching set of wide pleated trousers (*hakama*) and a jacket (*haori*), both of which had to be of a restrained and muted colour and should clearly display the clan badge or *mon* when on active duty in Edo. There was also a requirement for a particular form of mounting for swords, which should have black scabbards with metal fittings from the Gotō school of metalworkers. The scabbard of the katana had a squared-off tip and the wakizashi a more rounded one (plate 39). These all reflected the somewhat sober and Confucian outlook of the Tokugawa government, and an individual's personal taste in apparel and the mounting of swords could only be expressed when away from the shōgun's court in Edo.

Sankin Kōtai and early Tokugawa culture

To restrict even further the possibility of any potential threat to the shōgunate, the system of *Sankin Kōtai* was gradually introduced under which all of the provincial daimyō, both Fudai and Tozama, had to reside in Edo for alternate years or for alternate four- to six-month periods, to attend the shōgun. This system required that daimyō maintain both their provincial estates and residences in Edo, where their families were held as little more than hostages, with their movements severely restricted by the shōgunate. At first attendance was voluntary and seen as a gesture of good faith by the Fudai (and submission by the Tozama), but by 1635, under a revision to the Buke Sho-Hatto, attendance at Edo was made compulsory.

The cost of maintaining two residences and of organizing ceremonial processions (which were in theory strictly controlled) to and from Edo was a substantial drain on a daimyō's annual income. This was precisely what the shōgunate intended. A financially depleted daimyō was far less likely to present a challenge to the shōgun and it has been estimated that the expense of carrying out Sankin Kōtai accounted for as much as 80 per cent of a daimyō's annual income.

The processions of Sankin Kōtai were, however, an opportunity for the daimyō to display whatever personal wealth they had managed to retain, and although the shōgunate tried to regulate the numbers in these processions so that they had some relationship to the size of the particular daimyō's domain, in practice this was difficult to enforce. The size and splendour of the daimyō's cortege were recognized as an outward indication of his status, and these processions to and from Edo were frequently quite grand and dazzling affairs with the daimyō's retinue resplendently attired with fine armour and swords. Much of the armour of the Edo period was made purely for Sankin Kōtai or for other parade purposes and they became very ornate and non-functional as battle dress, since this was no longer a strictly necessary requirement.

Much of the parade armour of this time was increasingly being made of lacquered leather rather than iron, although the armour gave the outward appearance of a fully functional suit. Important defensive sections of these suits were still made of iron, and the helmets, the most important part of a suit of armour, were generally both a decorative and effective defence. These parade armours were relatively light and far more suited to processional marches, than to hard campaigning, particularly in the hot and humid climate of Japan's summers, when heavy armour, although efficient, was uncomfortable to wear. An incidental consequence of Sankin Kōtai was the stimulation of the nation's economy along the major routes to Edo which were being used very heavily by the daimyō and the officials of the shōgunate. In particular, the long-established coastal route known as the Tōkaidō (the route from Edo to Kyoto) flourished and many ancillary services grew up along its length.

The burdensome requirement of additional residences in Edo for the provincial daimyō, their families and retinue resulted in a rapid increase in economic development for this former fishing village. Artisans, labourers, craftsmen and tradesmen thrived with the greatly increased demand for their services. As with the jōkamachi of the Muromachi period, so Edo at this period attracted the best in all the services that the traditional craftsman could offer. Although craftsmen ranked lower in the social order than farmers, those whose talents were of particular use to the military authorities were at least accorded some respect and were treated far better than other artisans. In particular, armourers and swordsmiths were frequently directly employed by the shōgunate. Some artisans were even given the right to carry one sword and were almost, but not quite, granted samurai status. Others who were directly employed either by the shōgunate or by a daimyō usually received little salary, but were at least assured of a market for their services (plate 40).

The fact that the Buke Sho-Hatto forbade the further development of castles (allowing only repairs) only served further to increase the flow of craftsmen to the city. The shōgun, however, developed his own castle in Edo into a magnificent symbol of power and authority, and Edo Castle became the central focus both of the developing new metropolis and of the country itself. Alongside the mansions and palaces of the daimyō (which are reckoned to have accounted for up to 60 per cent of the available urban land in Edo) the workshops of the artisans and the shops of the merchants developed together with (in a relatively short period of time) the pleasure quarters, which were eventually regulated by the shōgunate. It is somewhat ironic to note here that Edo Castle, the centre of authority of the Tokugawa family, became the new imperial palace following the overthrow of the shōgunate in the mid-nineteenth century.

40 A bow maker illustrated in the anonymous, 18th-century, woodblock-printed book *Shokunin Uta Awase* (Poetry Competition on the Theme of Craftsmen). Interestingly, he is shown wearing a short sword while carrying out his trade. V&A: E.2705–1925.

Art and culture flourished under the Tokugawa shōgunate, although often this was in effect little more than the continued patronage of those genres, schools or styles of painting, architecture and drama which had enjoyed shōgunal patronage throughout the Muromachi period. Despite the many restrictive laws passed by the shōgunate, foreign studies did develop, known as *rangaku*, and included medicine as well as the arts. Chinese-style literati painting was popular as it reflected the stern Confucian philosophies adopted by the Tokugawa shōguns, and these philosophies and associated aesthetic tastes in the arts gradually spread to the populace as a whole. The maintenance of castles and the existing castle towns presented further opportunities for the creation of gardens and outdoor stages for Nō performances, which along with the Tea Ceremony were perpetuated as the prerogative of the ruling military elite. We see once again the adoption of tastes by the ruling military which were perhaps more suited to the aristocrats of court than to a class which has its roots in warrior traditions.

The enforced peace of the period created the opportunity for new developments in the production of porcelain, lacquer, metalwork and textiles, which found a ready market for the now increasingly leisured and more culturally minded samurai class. It also created an environment in which the merchant classes greatly prospered, and they would, in time, become more significant in both Edo-period society and in the arts as the new patrons with the wherewithal and willingness to pay for exquisitely finished works of art of all forms.

Shintō, 'new swords'

The sword was still as important as ever to the samurai both as a weapon and symbol of authority, and we have already seen how the Tokugawa shōgunate, through the instructions laid down in the Buke Sho-Hatto, insisted that the samurai continue to study the military arts. With the arrival of the Europeans had come new forms of technology which had helped increase the local production of steel as well as the direct importation of cheap foreign, or *namban*, iron. Steel production became simpler, more efficient and cheaper, and the demand for blades was still particularly strong, although there were now no longer any major battles to be fought. The samurai were still the only group permitted to carry the two swords of the daishō, but others such as doctors, priests and later merchants were, under strict regulations, permitted to carry a single short sword.

Swords following the pattern of the cut-down swords from earlier periods continued to be made by schools of the Gokaden, particularly those of Bizen, Mino and Sagami. A newer development in the early Edo period was that of blades which had a very slight curvature or which were almost straight but narrowed in width towards the tip. These swords were known as Kambun shintō after the period (1661–73) in which they first began to appear. Various theories have been suggested for this change in shape. One was the convenience of carrying a straighter sword, although the requirement for a saki-zori curvature of a blade would seem even more suited to the continuous drawing and cutting action required of a sword worn without armour in an urban environment.

Perhaps another reason for this transformation of shape was due to the establishment of dedicated schools (dōjō) of traditional sword fencing, *kendō* (the way of the sword). Schools of kendō developed as a direct result of the establishment of peace in Japan and the resulting lack of any real opportunity to use the sword in battle. Many of the schools of kendō were established by rōnin who were keen to maintain their martial traditions. Sword fighting techniques became somewhat formalized and ritualized with some schools of kendō developing fighting actions which utilized large, rounded cutting actions (plate 41).

There was a distinct difference between swords produced in and around Edo and those of Osaka, the two major cities of Japan at that time. Edo, being the centre of the shōgunate, inevitably produced swords with restrained characteristics more suited to the somewhat austere requirements laid down by the shogun's court. Osaka, on the other hand, being the centre of trade, commerce and industry in Japan, as well as being at some distance from Edo and nearer the influences of the imperial court at Kyoto, produced swords with more elaborate patterning, particularly on the hamon. The mountings of Osaka blades were also more lavish and ostentatious in keeping with the demands of the predominant merchant class of Osaka, who were rapidly becoming the new patrons of swordsmiths, and associated artisans, as their wealth soared in the peaceful and ordered climate of the Edo period. The regional domains of the daimyō also maintained and developed their own styles and traditions in swords and fittings, and the castle towns which had developed over the previous century still attracted many fine swordsmiths.

Many of the emerging smiths of Osaka were influenced by the Kyoto swordsmiths, who, though living and working within the physical sphere of the Yamashiro schools of Kyoto, had their own roots based in the traditions of the Sagami schools of Kamakura. Notable among the Osaka smiths were the pupils of Horikawa Kunihiro including such important swordsmiths as Kawachi no Kami Kunisuke and his son Naka Kawachi. He is credited with creating a form of chōji hamon called *kobushi gata*, 'fist-shaped' chōji, a style which was to be copied by later smiths of various schools (such as the Bizen Yokoyama smiths). Other Osaka swordsmiths of significance included those using the name Sukehiro from the Osaka branch of the Ishido⁻ school, which had specialized in early Bizen-style blades – especially Sukehiro II, who signed himself Tsuta Echizen no Kami Sukehiro. Sukehiro II originally made blades with the traditional chōji hamon of his school, but is credited with inventing the *tōran midare hamon*, 'billowing waves hamon', which he combined with jihada of bright ko-itame. This distinctive style appealed to the Osaka taste for flamboyance and showiness, a trait which some would say is still characteristic of Osaka and its people today (plate 42).

Perhaps the most renowned of the Osaka smiths in the seventeenth century was Izumi no Kami Kunisada II, more commonly known as Inoue Shinkai, a name meaning 'True Renewal' which he adopted on taking Buddhist orders around 1670. He produced many fine short swords with ko-itame hada and broad hamon of slightly undulating suguha or notare midare. There is much nie and nioi present in his blades as well as distinct patches of kinsuji. The connoisseur Kamada Gyōmyō, who lived at the end of the

41 Kendō practice from volume II of the *Hokusai Manga, c.*1816. Hokusai produced fifteen volumes of these woodblock-printed books between 1814 and 1878 and depicted many instances of martial arts being carried out. Although at this historical period armour would have been worn during kendō practice, Hokusai has chosen to show the fencers without any armour.
V&A: E.14863–1886.

eighteenth century and compiled various studies of both kotō and shintō blades, even went as far as to call Shinkai 'the Masamune of Osaka'. His work was of such high quality that he was given permission to carve the imperial chrysanthemum crest onto the tang of his blades.

In Edo the Ishidō school also flourished but produced blades which had more complex hamon than those of the other branches of the school, especially the Osaka branch. A characteristic of the blades of the Ishidō school was that of chōji hamon combined with a fine utsuri. The Echizen smith Yasutsugu came to Edo to produce swords for Tokugawa Ieyasu in the style of the blades of Sagami and was even asked by Ieyasu to make copies of blades by famous Sagami smiths. The *yasu* character (which can be written in several ways) of 'Yasutsugu' was changed from the original one to that used by Tokugawa Ieyasu, and this tradition of taking part of one's name from a superior was deemed a great honour. He was also given the privilege of carving the Tokugawa triple hollyhock crest onto the nakago of his blades and his successors maintained that right. His own swords have fine itame grain in the tempered areas of the blade and a complex grained jihada which contains plenty of jinie. Many of his blades, and indeed those of his son Yasutsugu II, also feature fine horimono, which were generally not carved by the smiths themselves but by specialist craftsmen. Both father and son were patronized by several generations of Tokugawa shōguns and worked both in Edo and in their home province of Echizen. Some Yasutsugu blades bear the inscription 'made with Namban iron' (plate 43).

Among other notable smiths working in Edo during the early part of the Edo period was Noda Hankei. Hankei

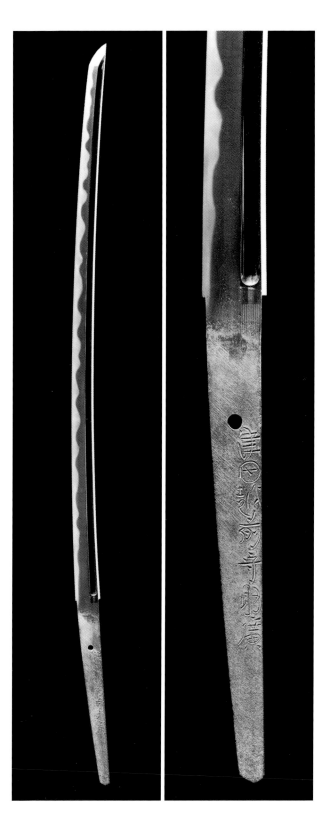

42 Katana blade signed 'Tsuda Echizen [no] Kami Sukehiro' and 'Empō go nen, hachi gatsu, hi' (a day in the eighth month of the fifth year of the Empō period [equivalent to 1677]). The Kambun shintō style is still evident in this sword made just after the end of that period. Sukehiro is credited with the development of the beautiful wide and deeply undulating tōran midare hamon, which can be clearly seen on this blade. This particular style of hamon was copied by many later Osaka smiths.

Collection of the Tokyo National Museum, Important Art Object.

43 Wakizashi blade signed
'Bushū Edo Echizen Yasutsugu'
(Yasutsugu of Echizen province,
at Edo in Musashi province).
Yasutsugu was court swordsmith
to the third Tokugawa shōgun,
Iemitsu. This blade is most likely
by the second smith to bear
the name of Yasutsugu, who
died in 1646.
V&A: M.24–1912.

was originally a gunsmith working for the shōgunate in Edo where he used the name Shigetaka. He left Edo in 1607 to return to his native town of Suruga where he continued to make guns but also began to produce swords. He returned to Edo in 1616 when Ieyasu died and set up as a sword maker using the name Hankei (plate 44). Hankei produced bold blades with bright jihada and with strong hamon featuring predominant sunagashi and kinsuji. The jihada of his blades exhibits large itame graining. He also developed a distinctively shaped nakago. He is alleged to have been found murdered in the streets of Edo in 1646 with his body cut in two, the assailant and the reason for the murder were never discovered.

Of particular note among the early smiths working in Edo was Nagasone Kotetsu. Kotetsu was originally a maker of armour working out of Fukui in Echizen province, but as the demand for good functional armour declined during the Edo period he changed to sword manufacture when aged fifty-one and moved to Edo. Inami Hakusui, who wrote the excellent book *Nippontō* in 1948, relates a splendid anecdote about why this change of profession came about. The story, as written by Inami, describes how a test was proposed in the presence of the Echizen daimyō to see what was more efficient, one of Kotetsu's helmets or one of the swords made by a smith whose name is given as Kiyomitsu. Kotetsu became unsure as to whether his helmet would survive the cut which was to be given by Kiyomitsu himself. A fraction of a second before Kiyomitsu delivered the cut to the helmet, Kotetsu called out and asked to rearrange the helmet on its stand. Kiyomitsu's composure was

44 Tantō blade signed 'Hankei' (Noda Hankei of Edo). The broad hamon with its distinctive lines of kinsuji and sunagashi (particularly noticeable here on the ura) are all indicative of the work of the former gunsmith Shigetaka, who turned his skills to sword making and began from about 1616 to use the name 'Hankei' (an alternative reading of the characters of his name and one by which he is generally better known). The omote has an unusual horimono of what appears to be a heron with a feather in its beak.

Collection of the Tokyo National Museum, Important Art Object.

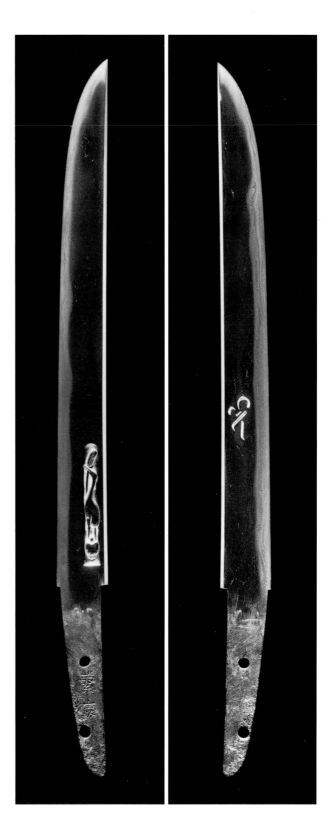

45 Katana blade signed
'Nagasone Kotetsu Nyūdo
Okisato' (Nagasone Kotetsu
Okisato the lay priest) and a
cutting inscription (tameshigiri)
dated equivalent to 1665, which
states that one Yamano Ka'emon
(known as Nagahisa) at the age
of 68 cut through four bodies
with this blade. Nagasone
Kotetsu was formerly an
armour maker and began his
sword-making career in Edo in
1656 when aged 51. The details
of this blade show many of the
characteristics found on
Kambun-period swords and the
gently notare hamon with rich
nioi is typical of Kotetsu's work
of this period.

Collection of the Tokyo National
Museum.

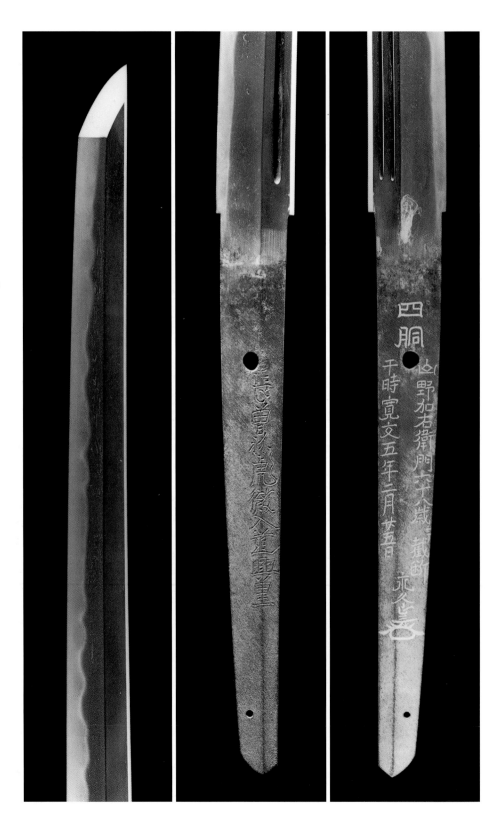

shattered and his ensuing cut merely penetrated a small section of the helmet. Kotetsu was so ashamed of his behaviour that he apologized and remorsefully left his home province to pursue the study of sword making (plate 45).[4]

Whatever the reason for the change of profession, Kotetsu's blades were soon in demand and they quickly gained a reputation for their excellent cutting abilities as well as their aesthetically pleasing finish. His early blades were in the Nambokuchō style and the hamon were of gunome, notare and suguha. He is credited with the introduction of the gunome hamon known as *juzuba*, 'rosary hamon', as the regular heads of the hamon resemble a row of rosary beads. Perhaps due to his experience as an armourer many of his blades carried finely worked horimono of Sanskrit characters and various deities. He became so renowned that even during his relatively short career as a sword maker (*c*.1656–78) unscrupulous smiths were faking his work. Many of his genuine extant swords bear inscriptions attesting to the cutting efficiency of his blades, which were tested by professional appraisers.

Blade appraisal and the Hon'ami family

The Japanese sword had for centuries been appreciated not only for its cutting efficiency but for the intrinsic beauty of its metallurgical qualities. As far back as the tenth century the *Engi Shiki* (Record of the Engi Period, AD 901–22) refers to the techniques required for polishing a blade, which indicates that the surface finish of a sword was at least worth considering. A book dating from 1316, the *Kanchi-in Bon* (so-called after the building in the Tōji Temple where it was kept), was dedicated to the study of the various smiths and their respective schools and exemplifies the earliest methodical examination of the Japanese sword. The *Kanchi-in Bon* also details those sword polishers and smiths in the group which accompanied the Emperor Go-Toba while he produced swords from exile.

The concept of the *meitō*, a 'sword with a name', evolved together with an appreciation of the sword as an art object. Although fine swords had long been admired both as effective weapons and for their aesthetic qualities, it was really only in a time of relative peace that it was possible for connoisseurs to develop and codify their theories on what constituted a meitō. To be regarded as a meitō the sword does not necessarily have to be signed, although this is an important consideration. It must, however, be well forged with a good shape and demonstrate successfully the characteristics associated with the particular school or smith to whom it is attributed. The blade should not be altered in any significant way, although of course many early swords had been shortened, re-ground or re-tempered as a result of battle damage, or generally repolished. These are all processes which can alter the physical shape and visual appearance of a blade. The sword should also, preferably, have a history, that is be associated with a particularly notable family, individual or event.

In the Edo period the Tokugawa shōgunate appointed the Hon'ami family as their official group of sword appraisers, the *mekiki*. The Hon'ami had long been involved with swords and the arts and had been officials under the Ashikaga shōguns. Under Hon'ami Saburōbei Kōtoku (1554–1619) the family were given the official title of *Tenka no Tōken Mekikijo*, 'National Office for Sword Appraisal'. They had been part of a group of officials who regulated the arts and crafts and all used the Japanese character for *ami* in their names. The character for *hon* in Hon'ami can be read as 'original', the use here indicating a long pedigree, real or invented.

The official appointment of the Hon'ami by the Tokugawa shōgunate came as recognition of the illustrious Hon'ami Kōetsu who was renowned in the fields of painting, lacquerware, ceramics and the Tea Ceremony. The Hon'ami originally provided certificates of authenticity for swords which had lost their signatures or were unsigned but attributed to a particular smith. They were later employed in the cutting down of the long early swords which were remounted in the style and taste of the current period. As part of the attribution process they would often inlay the name of the smith, not however copying any recognized signature, as well as their own name, or simply the character *hon*, together with their art seal (*kao*) in gold on the tang of the blade in question.

The issuing of these certificates of authenticity, while confirming the aesthetic merits of a blade together with its history, had the effect of changing the market value of particularly desirable swords. It was also a potentially corrupt system and it is known that on several occasions dubious attributions of authenticity were made. Although no obviously corrupt motives can be assigned to the practice, it appears that the Hon'ami were at least 'flexible' on occasions. There are certainly far more blades in existence today which are attributed to Masamune and Sanjō Munechika (both extremely desirable swordsmiths) than could reasonably be expected (plate 46).

In 1611 the Hon'ami family published the *Kotō Meizukushi*, an appraisal of kotō blades by both province and school, and in 1719 were specifically requested by Shōgun Tokugawa Yoshimune to produce a list of the 'best' swords in existence at that time. The resulting work was named the *Kyōhō Meibutsu Chō*, the 'Catalogue of Famous Things'. The book listed all the known meitō in the collections of the Tokugawa family and the principal daimyō, but the emphasis of the book was on the Sagami school of sword makers and Bizen and the other schools are significantly neglected. These omissions perhaps reflected the prevailing taste in swords as dictated by the shōgunate as well as the Hon'ami predilection for cutting down Nambokuchō-period swords which had previously been attributed to pupils of Masamune.

The tang, or nakago, of a blade was where most inscriptions were carved and a wealth of information can be found there: not only the smith's name but the date and place of manufacture, the owner's name, dedicatory or admonitory inscriptions, the name of the horimono carver as well as cutting inscriptions. During a shortening process much or indeed all of the information can be lost, and even the simple act of drilling a new hole for the securing pin can obscure important information. The custom of inlaying the tang of shortened blades with a signature approved by an official sword-appraiser sometimes ignored the original style of sword, so that an old tachi blade could sometimes be inlaid with a katana-style signature, i.e. the signature would be away from the body when the sword was worn with the cutting edge uppermost.

There are ways of retaining the original signature of a sword, but when a blade is assessed, signature alone is insufficient information. For example, the style of signature known as *gaku-mei* can be misleading, as this is where an original signature has been cut out of an old blade during the shortening process and then reinserted into the tang of the same blade. It is equally simple to remove an authentic signature from a blade and have it inserted into a completely different and otherwise unremarkable sword. If,

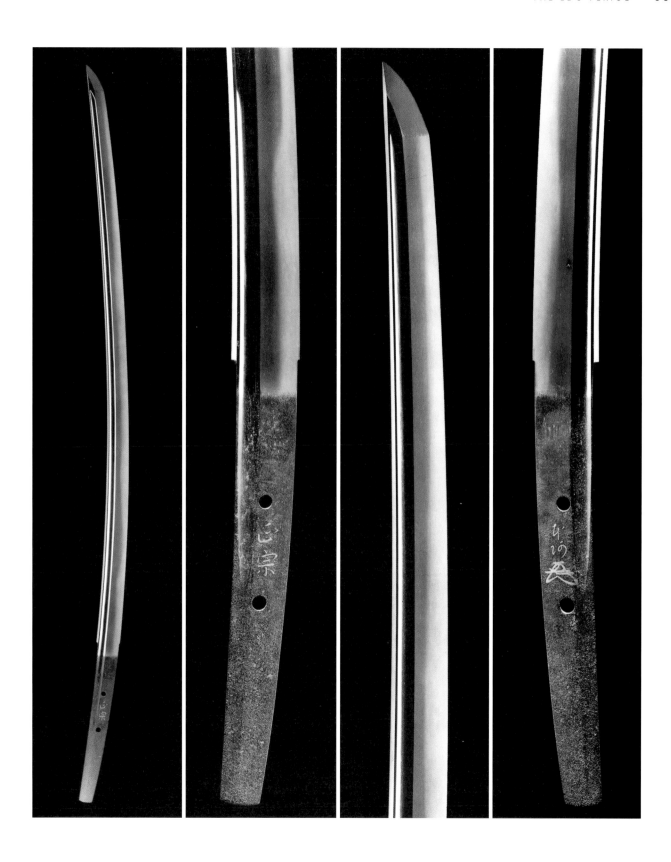

however, an original signature is inserted into the nakago of another blade, which bears many of the characteristics of the smith in question but is otherwise unsigned, and the original blade is inscribed with a new gold attribution signature, then immediately we have two blades by an important smith for the price of one! Forgeries and fakes have long been a difficult problem with the Japanese sword and there are many other ways of making a blade appear to be something which it blatantly is not. The simplest means is of course the direct copying of an original signature onto a fake blade or by the skilful (or otherwise) alteration of existing inscriptions on the tang (plate 47).

It can therefore be seen that the decisions involved in determining whether a sword is a meitō or not are vague and can often be extremely subjective. As Kanzan Satō, the twentieth-century authority on Japanese swords, wrote: 'Although a sword is in essence a meitō, conditions have to be attached.'[5] Connoisseurship, for better or worse and certainly as applied to the Japanese sword, is an inexact and somewhat subjective science. There are many blades in existence today which are in themselves fine and excellent swords but which are, through lack of signature or history, deemed 'inferior' to the 'great' swords. The Japanese national system of designation of art works, including swords, as 'Important Cultural Property' or 'National Treasure' is one full of speculation and arguments. Heated discussions about what deserves designation still rage regarding swords which have, or have not, received this form of national recognition. There is so much disagreement and infighting that individual Japanese prefectures can also have their own baffling local designations and there are even individual private collections (albeit in rather remote regions of Japan) with their own confusing classifications. Pedigree and recognition in Japan denote status (as well as a particular pride in heritage and the continuation of tradition), and these systems of designation and classification are always open to much controversy.

During the peace of the Edo period the samurai had little opportunity to prove either their fencing skills or the efficiency of their blades in battle. Schools of kendō had developed to test the former, and official blade appraisers were established to check the latter. The more respectable samurai took their blades to these professionals who tested them in various prescribed ways, the cutting attestations – *tameshigiri* – being inscribed on the tang of the blade. The blades assessed in this way were generally made by shintō smiths who needed to prove that their blades were efficient as well as beautiful objects. The swords were used on condemned criminals or their corpses, which were sometimes bundled together to increase resistance to the cut. Up to seven bodies at one time are alleged to have been cut through in a single blow. Swords were also tested on bundles

47 Katana blade with a fake signature 'Bizen Osafune ju nin Kanemitsu' (i.e. the renowned 14th-century smith) and 'Embun nana nen, ni gatsu hi' (second month of the seventh year of the Embun period [equivalent to 1362]). It is obvious that the final two characters of the signature have been altered, as have the first two of the date. Tellingly, the Embun period (of the brief Northern dynasty) lasted only five years. The characteristics of the blade and the style of the original signature are most likely those of either Sukenaga (1795–1851) or Sukekane of the Yokoyama school of Bizen, and the only historical period of seven years or more which fits this hypothesis is Tempō (1830–44), which would make the actual date of the blade 1836.
V&A: M.7–1947, Jahn Bequest.

48 Blade with a cutting inscription (tameshigiri) 'Futatsu dō, Tenwa ni, Inu, Ku gatsu, Tameshi Shō Yo' ([cut through] two bodies, second year of Tenwa, dog [year] ninth month, a true cutting test). Tenwa 2 is equivalent to 1682 and the blade is signed 'Kaga [no] Kami Fujiwara Morimichi'.
V&A: M.74–1922, Given by Mrs Biddulph in accordance with the wishes of the late Col. John Biddulph.

of wet straw (which has the same resilience as the human body) or on thick sections of bamboo (plate 48).

This custom of testing swords was observed and commented upon by the Portuguese Jesuit priest João Rodrigues in his *História da Igrejia do Japao* in the early seventeenth century:

> They [the Japanese] ... show great pity and compassion [for the killing of animals] but they do not feel this when they kill men in a bloodthirsty way and test their swords on corpses. Some lords may ask other nobles for some men who have been condemned to death in order to see whether their sword cuts well and can be trusted in emergencies. They often sew up bodies which have been cut up by swords and put together the severed parts so that they may once more cut. The delight and pleasure which they feel in cutting up human bodies is astonishing...[6] (plate 49)

The samurai had always possessed the unquestionable right to cut down anyone of lower rank who had offended them in any way. Article forty-four of the 'Code of 100 Articles' (sometimes mistakenly called the Legacy of Ieyasu, but actually written around 1650, more than thirty years after his death) gave legal permission for this action. This was defined under the term *kirisute gomen*, 'to cut down and leave'. However, some samurai, particularly those who had become rōnin, used to test their blades on innocent passers-by in the practice known as *tsuji-giri*, 'cutting at the crossroads'. This practice, although officially prohibited, was carried out with alarming regularity during the Edo period, particularly in cities which attracted certain types of undesirables as well as those rōnin who had developed into a criminal underclass. Bodies were left to be cleared away by the 'untouchable' class, the *Eta*, as even reporting the discovery of such a crime carried with it guilt by association and suspicion of the murder would fall on the individual who reported finding the body. It is thought that the swordsmith Hankei may well have been a victim of tsuji-giri.

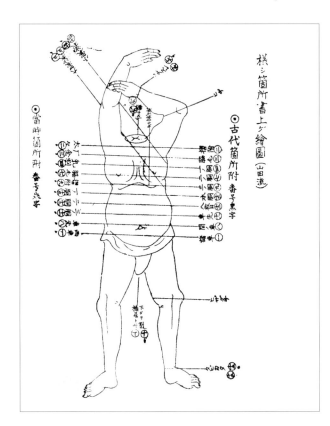

49 Tameshigiri according to the Yamada family. This diagram (together with many related documents) was given by Yamada Gengorō to Ishino Tamisaburō, sword-keeper to shōgun Tokugawa Ienari, in 1792 and illustrates the various prescribed cuts that could be carried out when testing a sword on a corpse. From Joly and Hogitaro, *Swords and Samé*, p.123.

The rōnin in Edo-period society

Many rōnin had been created during the early years of the Tokugawa period as a result of the Battle of Sekigahara, where their lord had been defeated or disgraced and thereby deprived of vassals and chattels, or through one of the many restrictions imposed by the shōgunate on daimyō limiting the number of samurai he could employ. Following the final crushing of the Toyotomi family at the fall of Osaka Castle in 1615 it has been estimated that some 500,000 rōnin were created. Some rōnin fitted into acceptable society, forming schools of kendō, entering holy orders or becoming (if well enough educated)

Confucian scholars, *jusha*. Others simply became mere vagabonds or grouped together in robber bands.

Some groups of townsmen on the fringes of society also formed gangs known as *otokodate*, 'self-disciplined men', or *kabukimono*, a word containing the meaning of eccentrics and deriving from the Japanese verb 'to swagger'. There were many early instances of these groups being led by samurai of *hatamoto* status. These were shōgunal vassals of high rank, below daimyō status but with a right of access to the shōgun himself. Many of the lower-ranking landowning hatamoto had been removed from the land and given an annual stipend by the shōgunate on condition that they resided in the jōkamachi. By the end of the seventeenth century nearly 90 per cent of hatamoto were living in cities on Tokugawa stipends, their lands having been added to that of the expanding Bakufu. Many gladly accepted this situation but, finding themselves without gainful employ, found other uses for their talents.

The kabukimono thought of themselves as protectors of the poor and upholders of justice and were romanticized in popular literature and later in plays as upholders of chivalrous values. They dressed in loudly patterned kimono, had outlandish hairdos, grew beards and wore large swords. Non-samurai kabukimono, who were not permitted to carry swords, used large iron war-fans or long metal smoking pipes, both of which could be used as effective weapons. This group of idealistic and armed individuals, and in the case of former samurai also well trained in the military arts, were potentially a great problem to the shōgunate and many degenerated into groups of organized criminality in the cities. As the groups began to get out of hand and were involved in murder, robbery and street-fighting, so the authorities began to clamp down and even greater restrictions were enforced on movement throughout the country.

The shōgunate fears of potential insurrection by the rōnin were nearly realized when in 1651 a rōnin-led conspiracy to overthrow the government was discovered. One of the two main ringleaders of this conspiracy was Yui Shōsetsu, a man of peasant stock who had been befriended by rōnin when a child and who aspired to follow the example of Hideyoshi, another peasant who had, through his natural abilities and ambitions, in time become ruler of Japan. The other ringleader was Marubashi Chūya, a samurai of good stock who had become a rōnin after his father was executed following the fall of Osaka Castle and who had long sought revenge on the Tokugawa family. Both men became teachers of the military arts and profited from the rules of the Buke Sho-Hatto which directed that all samurai study the arts of war as well as peace. The schools of military arts attracted many samurai of different classes, from minor daimyō to rōnin, and it was not surprising that some schools became places where grievances and complaints about the Bakufu could be aired by like-minded military men. A plan was hatched to explode gunpowder in a government magazine and in the ensuing conflagration in Edo, which had always been subject to disastrous fires, to seize Edo Castle, murder high officials and take control. Similar plans were laid for simultaneous action in other major cities in Japan.

The plot was discovered when Chūya became ill and revealed the scheme in his feverish ramblings. The leaders of the conspiracy were rounded up and they and their families were executed. The government, however, realizing that the plot was instigated mainly on behalf of unemployed samurai, decided not to try and use force against the remaining discontented rōnin throughout the country, but to somehow integrate them into society. There was a relaxation of some of the regulations on employing those rōnin who were deemed suitable to fit into society, and many former rōnin rose to become influential scholars and educators who expounded the traditional warrior ethics of the samurai. It was due in no small part to these individuals that an intellectual warrior ethos evolved which in time became known as *Bushidō*, 'the Way of the Warrior'.

The development of Bushidō, 'the Way of the Warrior'

One of the greatest exponents of the warrior ethos, before it became codified in bushidō, was Miyamoto Musashi (1584–*c*.1645). Musashi was himself a rōnin, having fought on the losing side at Sekigahara, but later on the winning side at Osaka Castle. Musashi was unhappy with the demise of the martial spirit and the way in which the samurai seemed to be becoming opportunistic individuals with little or no respect for the traditional martial values. Musashi was a master swordsman and devotee of Zen Buddhism and wrote the famous treatise on strategy and the arts of war, *Go Rin no Sho*, 'A Book of Five Rings', which is both a manual for the physical aspects of sword fencing and a philosophical work on the required mental attitudes to fighting. In this book he wrote:

> To attain the Way of strategy as a warrior you must deeply study fully other martial arts and not deviate even a little from the Way of the Warrior. With your spirit settled, accumulate practice day by day and hour by hour. Polish the twofold spirit heart and mind and sharpen the twofold gaze, perception and sight. When your spirit is not in the least bit clouded, when the clouds of bewilderment clear away, then there is the true void.[7]

When fighting, Musashi advocated the Zen principles of complete emptiness and used Zen terms such as *munen*, 'no thought', and *mushin*, 'no mind'. Once this state of spiritual awareness had been achieved, then the warrior could fight unhindered by emotion.

As well as being an important work on martial attitudes, this document recorded the results of many of the rapid social changes which the samurai in early seventeenth-century Japan were undergoing. It entreated the samurai to maintain a physical and spiritual readiness in all circumstances. Musashi had developed his own particular form of fencing using two swords, *nitō-ryū*, which demanded strenuous mental as well as physical techniques. According to Musashi, the attitude of the samurai, in whatever situation he found himself, should be complete acceptance of one's fate. Musashi wrote:

> Generally speaking, the way of the warrior is resolute acceptance of death... The warrior is different [from others] in that studying the Way of strategy is based on overcoming men. By victory gained in crossing swords with individuals, or enjoining battle with large numbers, we can attain power and fame for ourselves or our lord. This is the virtue of strategy.[8]

There had always been a conflict between the requirements of the warrior and the principles of Buddhism and Shintōism. Buddhism forbade the taking of any life, and Shintōism is particularly concerned with purity, so death and blood were regarded as especially defiling. In addition, the Confucian principles of loyalty were problematic, as establishing priorities was very difficult; for example, should a samurai's first loyalty lie with his father or his lord? The warrior's life should be spent in devotion to duty on behalf of his master and he must be ready at all times to lay down his life or kill for his lord. The samurai accepted with fortitude this condition and his every thought was concerned with matters of life and death. In the Edo period many philosophical works were written which dealt with the condition of the samurai. It can be argued that it is only in a time of peace that the warrior can truly reflect on this condition.

An anonymous early seventeenth-century treatise, *Heihokadenshō* (A Book of Strategy and Tactics in Victory and Defeat, *c*.1630), voiced some of the concerns about the samurai who took life, but justified their actions when carried under the correct, or at least morally approved, circumstances:

> The fighting man is an ill-omened instrument: the Way of Heaven has no love for him, yet has to make use of him, and this is the Way of Heaven… Ten thousand people are oppressed by the wickedness of one man, and by killing that one man the other ten thousand are given new life. So there the sword which kills is indeed the sword that gives life. There is righteousness in using the arts of fighting in this way. Without righteousness, it is merely a question of killing other people and avoiding being killed by them.[9]

With peace established in Japan after centuries of warfare, the ruling samurai class found themselves in the complicated position of having no more battles to fight, but under strict government orders to maintain their warrior traditions. Many samurai were, of course, employed ruling in the provinces, but many others, particularly in the large cities, found themselves idle, and the class became somewhat anomalous, although their right to rule was never questioned (plate 50). Under the relatively stable Tokugawa shōgunate and the prevailing intellectual climate of the times there evolved codes of behaviour founded on both Confucian beliefs and the Japanese tradition of absolute loyalty and willingness to die for one's master. This led to the development of the concept of bushidō.

The term *shidō*, with reference to a 'way of the warrior', was originally used by the neo-Confucian scholar Yamaga Sokō (1622–85) in the first of many of his treatises which analysed the position of the samurai and described their duties and social obligations under the Tokugawa shōgunate. He was particularly concerned about the incongruous position of the samurai and questioned its non-productive nature. However, he justified it by citing the example which the samurai must present to the other three social classes – farmers, artisans and merchants. He wrote in the following terms:

> For a samurai, nothing is more important than duty… The business of the samurai consists in reflecting on his own station in life, in discharging loyal service to his master if he has one … and with due consideration of his own position, in devoting himself to duty above all… Within his heart he keeps to the way of peace, but without he keeps his weapons ready for use. The samurai thus dispenses with the business of farmer, artisan and merchant, and confines himself to practising this Way.[10]

Sokō's lectures on the military sciences, combined with his deep understanding of both Buddhist and neo-Confucian ideology within the constraints of a peaceful national state, attracted large audiences which even included some daimyō and hatamoto. Sokō was only too aware of the problems faced by the samurai as they tried to combine their martial attributes with the demands of civil administration or simply find ways of fitting into a peaceful daily routine. However, he knew that if they were not to become

50 'Pictorial Representations of Popular Sayings', c.1867, by the eccentric late 19th-century artist Kawanabe Kyōsai. The caption beside the tree reads 'Cherry blossom is the best flower', that beside the younger samurai 'warrior is the best form of man' and that beside the elderly samurai 'Dango [dumplings] rather than cherry blossom'.
V&A: D.1375–1897.

totally redundant then they must find a place in the service of the shōgunate. He himself found practical employment for his skills and was military instructor for Asano, the daimyō of Akō province, but returned to Edo and produced a work which was critical of neo-Confucianism, resulting in his exile back to Akō. His wish was that the educated class of samurai would apply their traditional ideals of loyalty to the newly emerging nation state and take an active part in the running of the nation's affairs.

Arai Hakuseki (1656–1725) was another exceptional man of his times. Born the son of a rōnin, he devoted his life to the maintenance of the samurai spirit and rose late in life to become one of Japan's greatest historians as well as acting as economic adviser to the shōgunate. A sign of the acceptance of this former rōnin was when he was given the rank of hatamoto in 1713 and when, a few years later in 1716, he was entrusted with the re-drafting of the Buke Sho-Hatto, the document which had, in its original version, done so much against the rōnin. His autobiography is fascinating not only for the detailed accounts of his personal achievements but for stories of his father's life which reflect both his own strong filial and Confucian devotion and his admiration of, and firm belief in, the samurai values of loyalty, restraint and martial skills. He portrayed his father as a man with old-fashioned ideals which he regarded as being those most appropriate for the samurai, particularly in the peaceful period in which he found himself: 'Not long after the civil wars when my father was still a young man, men were chivalrous and were accustomed to setting a high value on the nobility of spirit which is in contrast to the situation today.'[11]

Arai justified the position of authority of the military classes of Japan in his book *Dokushi Yoron*, 'A Reading of History', and he accounts for the inevitability of warrior rule in the following terms: 'Ever since the Middle Ages it was only the warriors who strove to be faithful and who risked their lives for what they believed to be right… it is therefore only right that those who have taken it upon themselves to do the honourable thing should be rewarded…'[12] It is, of course, not uncommon for those who have risen into a particular class on the strength of their own abilities to form extreme views and to perpetuate the system which had in the past actively dissuaded or even persecuted them, and in this Arai, of former rōnin stock, was no exception.

The flourishing of Edo-period culture and the rise of the merchants

By the latter half of the seventeenth century most of those who had lived through the turmoil of Sekigahara and the storming of Osaka Castle were dead. The problem of the rōnin was mostly solved with their successive generations gradually fitting into society, although there were still many outcasts and villains to be found both in the countryside and in the cities. The population of the large cities had begun to settle into some kind of regular pattern of life and it was inevitable at this point that a new form of town-based culture would begin to flourish. The period from 1688 to 1704 bears the reign name of Genroku, a time when art, literature and the theatre all flourished, particularly in the major cities of Kyoto, the old capital with a long history of culture and refinement and still the seat of the powerless emperor; in Osaka, the traditional centre of commerce; and in Edo, the new capital with no real history or traditions.

The poet Bashō lived at this time, and both samurai and merchant aficionados of poetry patronized him. The wild extravagances of the kabuki theatre became popular with the townspeople (*chōnin*) and the samurai (who were entreated by the authorities to stay away from anything so vulgar). Kabuki was for a period overshadowed by the puppet theatre of Bunraku which flourished in and around Osaka. The themes of many of the plays of both Kabuki and Bunraku concerned the conflict between duty and passion experienced by the samurai in the great cities of Japan. The samurai were also among the regular visitors to the licensed pleasure quarters of the Yoshiwara in Edo where they increasingly mingled with the chōnin and the merchants.

Woodblock prints, especially books, did more than anything to help create and perpetuate the culture of *ukiyo*, the 'Floating World'. Prints were cheap to produce and had a readily available market. The subject matter of the Floating World depicted famous courtesans and beauties, singers, actors and increasingly the famous kabuki players. They gave an image of a world of leisure to which many aspired, but few could afford, although this was increasingly becoming less the case. The prints themselves began as black and white editions, but became more and more luxurious, so that by the late eighteenth century they had become art forms in themselves and the artists who produced them were well known. The Genroku period also saw the establishment of what is known as *iemoto*, 'house heads'. This was a system, prevalent in Japan to this day, whereby hereditary masters of those lineages which carried out the traditional Japanese leisure pursuits, such as tea, poetry, flower arranging, calligraphy, kendō and *kyudō* (archery), gave instruction, for a fee, in their specialist arts. Both samurai and the increasingly affluent and influential merchant class attended these classes, where the distinctions between the social orders were somewhat blurred.

The merchants were becoming the new patrons of the arts as it was generally thought demeaning for a samurai to concern himself with money. The samurai, now living in the cities rather than the countryside, had to adapt to their new conditions and it was inevitable that they should be forced to broaden their social horizons, but this was not without problems. There were occasional clashes between the samurai and towns-people, particularly in Kyoto and Osaka where the military classes had never been particularly respected and were seen to be constantly interfering with culture and commerce in the two respective cities. The prestige of the warrior class was seen to be gradually diminishing, as the profits made by the merchants caused inflation which badly affected those samurai eking out their existence on a fixed government stipend. The samurai were still, however, at the top of the social hierarchy introduced by Hideyoshi and had more rights than any other member of society at the time.

The merchants had long benefited from the military classes as contractors and suppliers for the campaigning during the Sengoku Jidai. Osaka merchants in particular had made huge profits as contractors for Hideyoshi and his ill-advised campaigns in Korea. During the time of the Tokugawa shōgunate they served as official government contractors and through their long-established networks, which had survived the warring periods, became indispensable to the military government. The samurai, who were all on fixed stipends and, in the case of daimyō, had to maintain two residences under Sankin Kōtai, became financially indebted to merchants and money-lenders. Some merchants flaunted their wealth to the irritation of the military authorities, who demanded moderation among their own class. This led to action by the shōgunate, who in one particular instance confiscated the entire estates of the merchant Yodoya family of Osaka.

The 'Forty-Seven Rōnin'

A series of incidents which occurred between 1701 and 1702 served to focus the authorities' attention on various issues which concerned the honour of the samurai while potentially questioning social order. The Akō Incident is better known as the 'Forty-Seven Loyal Rōnin' or *Chūshingura*, the 'Treasury of Loyal Retainers'. This series of events served as an inspiration for countless images in woodblock prints as well as for plays and romances, so much so that the original facts may have become somewhat distorted. The historical events are that in 1701 Asano Naganori, daimyō of Akō, was provoked into attacking Kira Yoshinaka while at the shōgun's court. The reasons for the provocation were unclear, but insults or requests for bribes by Kira are thought to have been the cause. Kira was not fatally injured, but Asano was arrested and executed, or rather obliged to commit *seppuku*, ritual suicide through disembowelling, on the same day as the attack, since the seriousness of his actions within the shōgun's court warranted such immediate retribution.

Seppuku, also known by the more vulgar term of *hara-kiri*, 'belly-slitting', was reserved as the honourable way for a samurai to atone for wrongdoing, real or presumed. It was a particularly painful form of death and was generally preceded by the writing of a

51 Left sheet of a triptych, *c*.1851, by the artist Kuniyoshi (renowned for his warrior prints), vividly depicting the famous night attack of the forty-seven rōnin on the house of Moronao (Kira). The cartouches in red identify the six particular rōnin who carried out the attack. V&A: E.11277–1886.

valedictory poem. The act would be carried out with great solemnity in a prescribed area and the accused would perform the actual incisions with his wakizashi or tantō, which would have the hilt wrapped in white paper. The first recorded historical instance of such an act was in 1170, when Minamoto Tametomo performed the act rather than be taken alive by his enemies. During the Edo period the provision of a *kaishaku-nin*, or 'second', became established. The second would cut off the head of the accused once he had made the first incision. On occasions the accused would be beheaded by his second as he reached forward for his dagger. It was regarded as more honourable to carry out the full act of seppuku, dying slowly, some even writing their valedictory poem in their own blood, an act which was regarded as highly admirable.

Following Asano's execution, the shōgunate immediately demanded the seizure of his estates, but many of his former retainers wanted to resist by force or to follow their lord into death through the practice known as *junshi*. This was another ancient tradition from a time when the bonds between lord and liege were extremely strong, and the retainer, or retainers, usually senior figures, carried out this act as a mark of respect, especially if they thought that their master had been forced to commit seppuku unjustly. The shōgunate banned this practice in an amendment to the Buke Sho-Hatto of 1663 but it certainly continued until 1668 when, following an act of junshi by a retainer of Okudaira Tadamasa, a minor daimyō, the retainer's children were executed, his remaining family exiled and the heir of Tadamasa was sent to a minor fiefdom. Despite this example there were many further instances of this barbaric practice.

Asano's retainers sent a petition to the Bakufu requesting that Asano's younger brother be appointed heir, as serving a direct heir of a deceased lord was acceptable to a warrior. The fiefdom was, however, surrendered while the Bakufu considered their request. This was eventually refused with the result that Asano's former retainers were now officially rōnin. It was theoretically possible for them to ask the authorities to give permission for an official vendetta, *katakiuchi*, against Asano's enemy Kira, a process which was permitted under the Buke Sho-Hatto, but they were fully aware that under the circumstances it would never be permitted. The retainers, led by Ōishi Yoshio, planned their revenge on Kira and for the next two years they appeared to have separated, outwardly leading a life of debauchery. In 1702 the retainers regrouped and carried out a sudden night attack on Kira's mansion in Edo, declaring as the attack commenced that this was katakiuchi, a private matter, so no neighbours came to Kira's help and he was cut down (plate 51). The forty-seven rōnin then presented Kira's head at their former lord's tomb in the small temple of Sengakuji and gave themselves up to the authorities.

Through their loyal actions they became immediate popular heroes, and not only among the common people, for as a sign of respect and admiration some were received personally into captivity by Hosokawa, the highly important daimyō of Higo province. Asano's men had broken civil law by their actions, but through their revenge on Kira had carried out the most important duty a samurai had, that of total loyalty to their master under any circumstance. Their actions were in complete contrast to the prevailing hedonistic atmosphere of the Genroku era when many thought that the samurai virtues had all but disappeared. In recognition of both their actions and widespread popular opinion, they were permitted to commit seppuku, an honourable death for a samurai and one which strictly speaking was not permitted to rōnin.

They were buried alongside Asano at Sengakuji and the graves can be seen there today, well tended and frequently with incense burning at Asano's grave. There is also a rather neglected little museum at the temple containing personal artefacts of the rōnin. Following their deaths, many plays were produced which told, in rather romantic terms, the story of loyalty and devotion to duty, and the subject was depicted in hundreds of different woodblock prints.

Swords in the later Edo period

During the generally peaceful eighteenth century there was a significant decrease in the production of swords which was inextricably linked to the fall in the real purchasing power of the samurai class, together with the almost complete decline in the demand for fine functional or stylish swords. There were certainly no blades produced which could remotely qualify as meitō. Few smiths of any great note produced fine blades, although the Gokaden, particularly the Mino school, continued to produce serviceable swords all over the country. Smiths such as Tamba no kami Yoshimichi produced good blades which were both efficient weapons and bore some distinctive artistic qualities. In contrast with the decline in sword production there was, however, a great increase in the demand for fine decorative sword fittings, particularly for those rich townsmen who had acquired the right to carry a sword, and there was no shortage of able craftsmen willing to produce these luxury items.

Shōgun Yoshimune (reigned 1716–45), the eighth and one of the ablest of the later Tokugawa shōguns, had in 1719 commissioned the *Kyōhō Meibutsu Chō*, the 'Catalogue of Famous Swords', and had smiths from Satsuma, an area long renowned for its martial spirit, come to Edo to make the strong bold blades in the Sagami style for which Satsuma smiths were famed. Yoshimune was also concerned about the apparent breakdown of the military structure of the country to the advantage of the ascending merchant classes and advocated a return to the principles of Ieyasu's rule through a general reduction at all levels of expenditure on luxury items. In 1724 he laid down particularly strict sumptuary regulations which, among other things, restricted showy fashions and the purchasing of expensive lacquerware. Many samurai were, of course, financially in no position to acquire such rich accoutrements and the regulations were indirectly aimed at the merchants who were prospering and overtly acquiring such luxuries.

Despite the many sumptuary rulings laid down by the Bakufu during the Edo period, many swords, notably from the Genroku period onwards, were increasingly being mounted in a particularly luxurious fashion, especially when away from the shōgun's court. Scabbards were richly decorated with fine lacquer and adorned with superbly crafted metal fittings. These were produced by the emerging studios of the *machibori*, the town carvers of soft metal sword fittings who were not restricted by the styles required for the daishō which had to be worn at the shōgun's court (plate 52). The court styles of fittings were produced by the Gotō school of metalworkers, the *iebori*, the 'house', or 'family carvers' as they were known. The Gotō school had been in shōgunal service since the Muromachi period under Ashikaga Yoshimasa (1435–90) and had successively served under Nobunaga and Hideyoshi. Gotō Tokujō, the fifth of the line, was taken into service by Tokugawa Ieyasu and the Gotō school continued to make fittings

52 Tantō mounting, *c.*1800, in a wooden scabbard with decoration of dark matt and fine mother-of-pearl lacquer on a dark red ground; metal mounts of silver, with details in gold, all on the theme of Fuden and Raiden, the wind and thunder gods. The kogai has one of the deities in copper. The small tsuba is of russet-patinated iron with karakusa scrolling and pauwlonia inlay in gold. V&A: M.20–1947, Jahn Bequest.

for the Tokugawa family and those attending the shōgun's court until the imperial restoration in 1868.

The materials used for Gotō school sword fittings were restricted to *shakudō*, an alloy of copper and gold which is then patinated to a rich purple-black colour once described by Hideyoshi as having the colour of raindrops seen on a crow's wing. In addition to the materials to be used, the subject matter was also restricted and the fittings should, at some place, bear the mon, or clan badge of the wearer. These decorations were in low or high relief gold inlay. Sets of kozuka, kōgai and menuki made by the Gotō school were known as *midokoro-mono*, 'things for three places'. Under the Bakufu regulations the kashira of swords to be worn at the shōgun's court were not, however, metal but horn.

Many of the craftsmen of the machibori had broken away from the Gotō schools with whom they had previously been employed. Perhaps the most renowned and innovative of these craftsmen was Yokoya Sōmin (1670–1733). He is credited with the introduction of the *katakiribori* style of metal decoration. This was a superbly creative form of carving into metal which utilized an angular chisel to give oblique cuts with the appearance of the brush strokes used in *suiboku*, ink painting. The copper and silver alloy *shibuichi*, which could be patinated to a wide range of silvery greys and browns, also became popular at this time. The subject matter of sets of sword fittings would frequently be represented on all of the different metal parts; tsuba, fuchi-kashira, menuki, kojiri, kurikata, kozuka and kōgai. The potentially restrictive shapes of sword fittings actually presented a challenge to the metalworker and they were used to full effect to deal with a wide range of popular, historical and humorous subjects (plate 53).

Horimono became more extravagant and now rarely depicted the inspirational warlike deities and religious invocations of the earlier carvings on blades. Auspicious carvings of plum, pine and cherry blossom, the 'Three Friends of Winter', were increasingly to be found on blades. The *Shichifukujin*, the 'Seven Gods of Good Fortune', whose number included popular versions of martial deities, were also found on blades. The Shichifukujin particularly appealed to the financial preoccupations of the merchants who were by now permitted to carry one short sword and, as we have already seen, were becoming the new wealthy patrons of the arts.

At the shōgun's court the traditional styles of sword mounting, including the ito-maki no tachi and court-style kazari-tachi, continued to be used. In the Edo period we see yet again in the history and development of the ruling military classes of Japan an adoption of the costume, tradition and manners of the imperial court. As a now more leisured class, the senior ruling samurai were able to indulge themselves in more aesthetic pursuits such as the Tea Ceremony, calligraphy and in particular the Nō theatre. The Nō theatre had been patronized by the military since the time of shōgun Ashikaga Takauji at the end of the fourteenth century. In 1647 Tokugawa Iemitsu had decreed that all the traditions of Nō had to be maintained without variation, and the plays, music, costume and masks all became standardized. Nō became the official music and drama

53 Group of sword fittings: clockwise (from top left), kozuka depicting the Kabuki actor Danjūrō, *c.*1696–1769; pair of menuki in the form of a bow with arrows in a quiver, *c.*1700; pair of menuki in the form of the bodhisattvas Fūgen and Monju, *c.*1837–96; kozuka with three carp, *c.*1760–1829; tsuba and kozuka depicting the foxes' wedding, *c.*1830; fuchi-kashira with horses, *c.*1800; fuchi-kashira with butterflies, *c.*1820.

V&A: M.111–1928; M.138–1924, Marcus Gift; M.476–1916, Alexander Gift; M.1414–1931, Hildburgh Gift; M.33 & 34–1920; M.624–1911; M.63–1957.

of the shōgunate and was rarely to be seen by the common people. Bugaku, the ancient dance of the imperial court, was also adopted by the shōgunate and Bugaku ceremonies were performed to the memory of Ieyasu at his sumptuous shrine at Nikkō.

By the late eighteenth century the samurai had for the most part been absorbed into administrative roles in the cities or were eking out a living on Bakufu stipends in the cities. Some found part-time employment as minor artisans but all were increasingly finding their finances stretched. Some resolved this problem by adopting the son of a merchant or wealthy chōnin for a fee, thereby conferring upon him the still extremely desirable status of samurai. There were established fees for the purchase of different levels of samurai status, but it is indicative of the declining condition of the samurai that the status which many had previously fought so hard to maintain could now be sold to those with enough money. This is not to say that the samurai had totally lost their dignity and authority, but the change from a warrior to an administrative position was a hard one to come to terms with, and if the sale of their valued status could help them maintain their social position, then this had reluctantly to be accepted.

The culmination of samurai rule

Following the attempts by Tokugawa Yoshimune, together with his able advisers, to reinforce the rule of the shōgunate, Japan was subsequently governed by two ineffective shōguns, Ieshige (1745–60) and Ieharu (1760–86), along with powerful and corrupt Bakufu officials (with their own strong personal agendas). These individuals and a succession of civil insurrections coincided with a damaging series of natural disasters (volcanic eruptions and subsequent crop failures), all contributing to the rapidly continuing deterioration in the authority of the Bakufu and their control of the country.

Tanuma Okitsugu, son of a minor samurai, became page and later chamberlain under Ieshige and subsequently became the favourite of Ieharu, under whom he rapidly rose to become a major daimyō and eventually President of the Ruling Council of Elders. For almost twenty years from 1767 Tanuma influenced Bakufu policy while accepting bribes quite openly. He is reported to have said that 'gold and silver are more important than life and when a man whose wish to serve is so earnest that he offers bribes it proves his dedication'.[13] When it was once remarked upon that Tanuma had everything in life, a samurai is said to have tellingly observed that all he lacked was a sword or suit of armour bearing marks from the battlefield.[14] The samurai tradition (at least in high office) was by now extremely corrupt and Tanuma was simply a manifestation of all that was wrong with the Bakufu. He eventually fell from power under the increasing civil unrest of the period which saw rioting in Edo, Osaka and Kyoto.

In 1787, under the daimyō Matsudaira Sadanobu, a series of countrywide reforms known as the Kansei Reforms were introduced. These aimed to restore order both in the countryside and in the towns. Peasants who had fled to the towns were allowed to return to the countryside and work the land, and any samurai debts owed to merchants and money-lenders which were over four years old were repealed. This had the effect of temporarily relieving the pressure on some samurai but the merchants suffered to the extent that they refused to lend any more to many junior samurai, thereby inflicting even greater financial hardship. Sadanobu was an ardent neo-Confucianist and under his influence the country experienced a revival in nationalistic spirit and a return to things purely 'Japanese', rather than to those cultural values based on Chinese or Buddhist examples. This inspired the development of what became known as *Kokugaku*, 'National Learning'. Many people were attracted to the writings of Motoori Norinaga, whose forty-four-volume work on the Kojiki, the mythological history of Japan, encouraged the Japanese to became more aware of their own country as 'the Land of the Gods', and in this atmosphere nationalism and Shintōism flourished.

All these policies and new ideologies were, however, simply temporary measures which slowed down the ultimate decline in the shōgun's authority. The uneasy peace between the shōgun in Edo and the emperor in Kyoto (under whom the shōguns ruled in name) was beginning to crumble. The people were discontented with Tokugawa authority, its sumptuary laws, censorship in writing and the arts, its network of spies and continuous attempts to control people's daily life. In Kyoto there was a strong resentment against Edo's authority and an increasing respect for, and in some instances veneration of, the emperor. These loyalist feeling were to grow and in due course bring down the shōgunate and renew the authority of the emperor who, being regarded as a direct descendant of Shintō's major deity, the Sun Goddess Amaterasu Ō-Mikami, was himself a deity to be revered.

The nationalistic revival and swords as heirlooms

Around 1800 this revival of nationalistic spirit resulted in a sudden increase in the production of excellent swords which attempted to recreate blades in the style of Kamakura and Nambokuchō swords, all harking back to the Golden Age of the Japanese sword. The blades which were being copied were, for the most part, early blades which had been cut down and remounted in the Momoyama and Edo periods, rather than the original extremely long blades. Swords made from around this time are known as *shin-shintō*, 'new, new swords' or 'new revival swords'.

This rekindling of sword making was principally led by Suishinshi Masahide, (1750–1825) who together with his many pupils attempted, with some outstanding successes, to recreate the historical styles of the swords of the Gokaden, particularly of the Bizen and Sagami schools. Many of the swords of this period feature the large kissaki which are to be found on the swords of the Nambokuchō period and can at times be confused with genuine blades of that period which through shortening have lost their signature. Some blades of the early nineteenth century were of such high quality that occasionally they deliberately had their contemporary signatures removed and were passed off as genuine items of the great age of the Japanese sword.

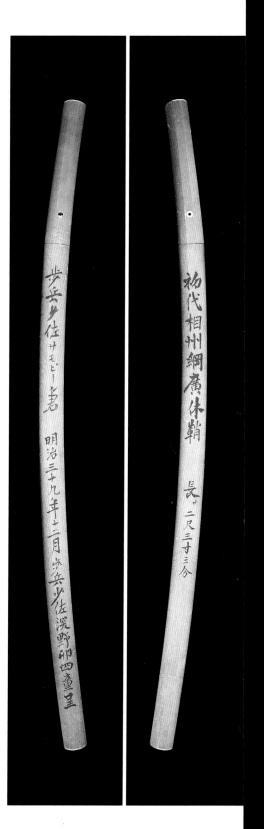

54 Shirasaya with ink inscriptions. On one side (right) the inscription reads 'Shodai Sōshū Tsunahiro Yasumizaya; nagasa ni shaku, san sun, san bu' (Tsunahiro 1st of Sōshū, 'resting' saya, length 2 shaku, 3 sun, 3 bu [approximately 71 cm]). The other side of the saya (left) reads 'Hoheishōsa Samubiru-kun, Meiji sanjukyu-nen, juni gatsu, Hoheishōsa Fukano Usushige tei' (respectfully given by Infantry Major Fukano Usushige to Infantry Major Somerville, twelfth month of Meiji 39 [=1906]'). Precisely what Somerville was doing in Japan at this time is at present unclear, but he later became British military attaché in Tokyo (see plate 35 for the blade from this saya).
V&A: M.356–1940, Gift of Colonel John C. Somerville, C.M.G., C.B.E.

55 Wakizashi blade signed on the omote 'Kashū ju Fujiwara Ietada' (Fujiwara Ietada of Kashū [Kaga]); on the mune 'Nihon Kaji Sosho Iga no Kami Fujiwara Kanamichi Kincho' (respectfully carved by Iga no Kami Fujiwara Kanemichi, Master Smith of Japan); and on the ura 'Jo-o san nen, hachi gatsu kichi jitsu' (a lucky day in the eighth month of the third year of Jo-o [equivalent to 1654]), 'Kunko Kaga no Kami mizukara tamawaru kore o' (a gift personally presented by the Daimyo and Lord of Kaga province), 'Imina Tadaaki-ko, Kansei san nen Kanoto I, Chuto juichi nichi' ([presented posthumously to] Lord Tadaaki on the eleventh day of the twelfth month, Pig year, third year of Kansei [equivalent to 1791]) and 'Sagami (no) Kuni (no) Omi; Yamazaki Hikoshirō Minamoto Yoshinao; Jinen niju-roku' (Yamazaki Hikoshiro Minamoto Yoshinao, aged 26, retainer of Sagami province). These inscriptions bear the mark of possibly three different hands. V&A: M.928–1916, Alexander Gift.

Not only swords reflected the styles of the earlier historical periods: armour was being made in the style of the Ō-yoroi, which was used during the Kamakura period. Sankin Kōtai continued and these early nineteenth-century parade armours featured various additions which would not have been found on early types, but the effect of the additional defences was purely ornamental rather than functional and historical accuracy was not of prime importance. The antiquarian style of the armour was sufficient to invoke the samurai's glorious military heritage of the earlier periods.

The fact that since early times the sword had remained of prime importance to the samurai, by the nineteenth century more as a symbol of status than as a weapon, explains why so many excellent swords have survived in Japan over the centuries. It had long been a tradition to give swords as gifts or as rewards for services rendered. There are stories, possibly apocryphal, but knowing the esteem in which many of the great smiths were held, probably true, of samurai accepting a meitō rather than financial reward. It was also a tradition that daimyō should present a new shōgun with an appropriate sword, i.e. a meitō. Mountings of the blade changed and older swords were altered, had horimono added or were cut down to suit the style of the period or an individual's preferences.

What needs to be stressed is that it is the blade which is important, not the mounting of the blade, which could be extremely plain yet hold an excellent blade, or gaudy and hold a worthless one. It was, and is, traditional that, when not mounted for use, the blade is stored simply in a *shirasaya*, a plain magnolia wood scabbard, which is often inscribed in black ink with the name of the smith, measurements of the blade and other details (plate 54). This being the case, the samurai could have several different mountings (scabbard, tsuba, etc.) for any one particular blade. He could even have the same blade mounted in the sombre style required at the shōgun's court and remounted in his own taste when away from court.

The shortage of genuine meitō during the Edo period meant that a blade which had apparently been shortened, but was at least in the style of a suitably acceptable smith, could be offered together with a certificate of authenticity, usually from the Hon'ami family. Sometimes the appropriate signature would also be added, either in gold with the Hon'ami seal or simply in the style of the relevant smith. This practice resulted in the existence of far more 'signed' or attributed blades by some of the more famous smiths than could possibly have been produced in their lifetime. However, as the blades had been presented as auspicious gifts, their authenticity was rarely questioned, the act of the presentation itself being considered honourable enough with no overt deception intended on the part of the donor.

Good blades held by samurai families were regarded as heirlooms and would be treated with great respect and carefully cleaned and oiled regularly. If a blade had a story behind it, for example if it had been used in battle or had been given by a high-ranking samurai, then it would be fully documented as such and many of these documents survive up to the present day (plate 55). Blades which were presented as offerings to shrines or temples and dedicated to the deities therein are also well documented. The important Shintō shrine of Atsuta Jingu, where the sword which forms part of the imperial regalia, Kusanagi no Tsurugi, is said to be enshrined, has a curious tradition of inscribing the dedication on the surface of the blade rather than on the tang. Today this shrine possesses swords which were dedicated as long ago as the Kamakura period.

6 | The Meiji Restoration and Beyond

The arrival of the 'Black Ships' and the downfall of the Shōgunate

By the early nineteenth century the shōgun had been effectively reduced to an almost powerless figure, real authority lying with the various interest groups involved in the actual governing of the country. From the early 1800s British and Russian ships were making new inroads into Japanese coastal waters making landings in direct opposition to the Japanese National Seclusion Policy, introduced in 1639. The Bakufu was beginning to hear stories about the strength of Western influence in the Far East, particularly the strength of their navies during the Opium Wars, and was being faced with further agrarian uprisings, rioting and insurrection at home including an attempted rebellion in Osaka. Hearing of the Chinese defeat by the British in 1842 at Nanking, regional daimyō had been encouraged by the Bakufu to build up their coastal defences, a scheme which only served to increase their own regional military strength and in turn contributed further to the destabilization of central government control. The arrival of the American Commodore Perry in Edo Bay in 1853 with a powerful squadron of ships in an attempt to open up trade, together with the ensuing increase in foreign contacts, put the shōgunal system under even greater threat as its policies crumbled under internal and external pressures.

In 1854 Perry returned with a still more powerful fleet, and a treaty was signed which opened up two ports to the Americans and allowed for an official consul. By the end of 1855 the British, Russian and Dutch governments had set up similar arrangements. Apart from the restricted Dutch trading base at Nagasaki, this was the first time for over two hundred years that the Japanese had directly encountered Westerners. What created one of the strongest impressions on the Japanese was the modern weaponry the Westerners brought with them, in particular revolvers and accurate artillery. The Bakufu resorted to consultation with the Fudai and Tozama daimyō about what should be done with the foreigners, thereby revealing their indecisiveness and weakness. They even went so far as to ask advice of the imperial court in Kyoto, an act which would have previously be unheard of. By 1859 further treaties allowed for foreign diplomats to reside in Edo itself, and Yokohama developed as a foreign settlement and trading port.

In the 1860s pro-imperial forces, notably from Satsuma and Chōshū, which had never been permitted to participate fully in national policy decisions, began to press for the full restoration of power to the emperor on the grounds that the Tokugawa shōguns were unfit to rule. The nationalistic feeling of the earlier part of the century had by now developed into the patriotic rallying cry of 'Sonnō Jōi!' – 'Revere the emperor, expel the barbarians!' The anger of the nationalists was also directed towards the Bakufu who

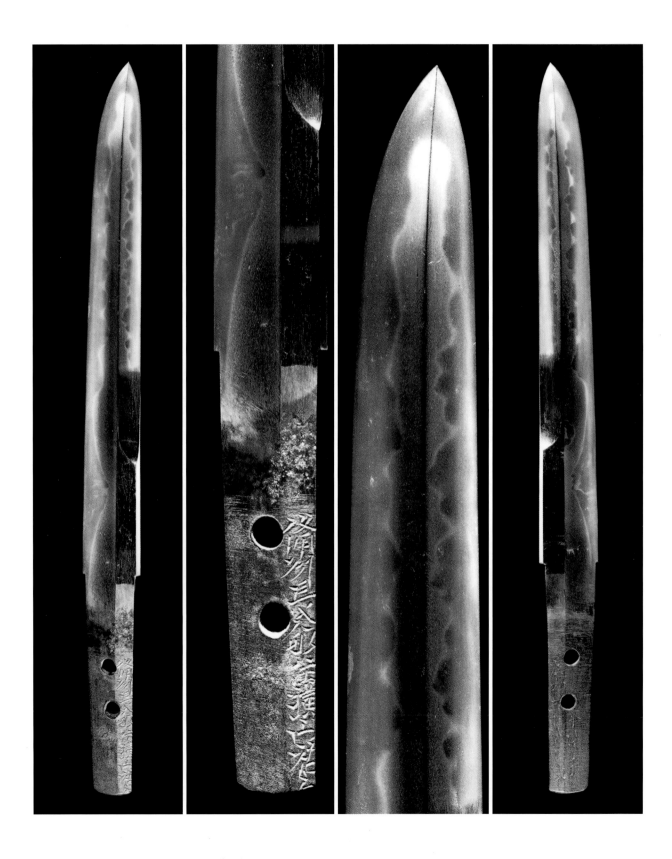

seemed to be acquiescing to all demands from the foreigners. Rival factions within the Tokugawa family, notably from Tokugawa Nariaki, the powerful daimyō of Mito but from a cadet branch of the Tokugawa family, sought the downfall of the Bakufu and actively plotted against it. The imperial court also encouraged dissent among the brooding daimyō against the government.

Sword manufacture continued throughout this period and many fine blades were produced by smiths such as Ishidō Korekazu (plate 56), who worked in the Bizen tradition, and Yamaura Kiyomaro, who made elegant blades in the Sagami tradition. Kiyomaro followed closely the work of Masamune and, after moving to Yotsuya in Edo, was dubbed 'the Masamune of Yotsuya'. The Yokoyama school of Bizen also produced fine large swords as well as elegant daggers with flamboyant hamon (plate 57). With mounting civil unrest there was once again an increase in the production of simple serviceable swords which were about to be used in battle on Japan's soil for almost the last time. Most of these blades were unsigned but followed the Bizen and Sōshū styles.

With the combination of pressure from the imperial court and the powerful daimyō, particularly those from Satsuma and Chōshū who were in open revolt, the Tokugawa Bakufu had no choice but to try and resist the threat to their 250-year-long rule of Japan. In 1864 Chōshū troops attempted to take control of the emperor in Kyoto, but they were beaten by Bakufu troops with the assistance of troops from Satsuma. The Bakufu then attempted to crush Chōshū, an ill-advised decision as Satsuma now provided assistance to Chōshū and the Bakufu troops failed in their attempts. In 1866 the shōgunate once again tried to subdue Chōshū and once again failed dismally, but the fatal illness of the reigning Shōgun Iemochi was timely and allowed the Bakufu forces to retire from a conflict which they were losing. The shōgunate had, for the first time, been defeated by the Tozama daimyō, a blow from which it was never to recover. Conscious of the tide turning against the shōgunate, Hitotsubashi Keiki (Tokugawa Yoshinobu) reluctantly assumed the mantle of shōgun only to relinquish all political authority to the emperor in November 1867, although retaining power as the head of a council of daimyō. In effect, an imperial restoration had already been made, but many did not accept the power which the Tokugawa family still managed to retain.

There were further minor acts of rebellion until in 1868 fighting took place around Kyoto itself between the Tokugawa forces and an 'imperial army' consisting of troops of the Satsuma/Chōshū alliance. The Tokugawa forces were defeated, and an imperial restoration was declared. There was continued fighting for some time after this in many parts of the country, as some Tokugawa forces refused to accept surrender, and for nearly a year there was a minor civil war. However, Edo surrendered without bloodshed and by 1869 the Emperor Meiji had established himself there in the shōgun's former castle; the city was renamed Tokyo. The samurai at that time formed about 5 per cent of the population of Japan but continued to receive government stipends which accounted for around 30 per cent of the annual budget.

Westerners in Japan

With foreigners beginning to take up residence in Japan and Sonnō Jōi being adopted by the masses, there were many attacks on the newcomers, particularly in Yokohama and especially by the rōnin who were still very much in evidence. Many rōnin saw this

57 Tantō blade signed 'Bishū Osafune Ju Yokoyama Suke[kane]' (Yokoyama Sukekane resident of Osafune in Bizen province) and 'Tomonari gojuhachi dai mago, … nen … gatsu hi' (58th generation grandchild [descendant] of Tomonari, a day in ?month of ?year), *c.*1860–70. The hamon depicting Mount Fuji with the sun on one side and the moon on the other together with a *ko-bushi* ('clenched fist') pattern features on several other tantō blades by Sukekane. Blades of the nineteenth-century Yokoyama school frequently declared their lineage as being directly descended from the thirteenth-century smith Tomonari.
V&A: M.1336–1926, Given from the collection of the late Ernest A. Brooks, of Cedarhurst, Long Island, USA.

time of unrest as an opportunity to re-establish their lost samurai traditions in the service of the emperor, rather than for the ineffectual Tokugawa family. In one particular incident in 1863 an English merchant, Charles Richardson, riding near Yokohama was attacked and killed by Satsuma samurai when he refused to show the samurai any respect. The British government then tried, to no avail, to obtain recompense from the Satsuma daimyō through the Bakufu, so the clan town of Kagoshima on Kyūshū was bombarded by British warships, an act which gained the grudging respect from the citizens who approved of such direct military action in the best samurai tradition.

Resentment against foreigners continued unabated, and in 1868 the British envoy, Sir Harry Parkes, and his entourage were attacked while on their way to an audience with the emperor in Kyoto. Parkes set out for the imperial audience on 23 March with his translators A.B. Mitford and E. Satow and an escort of British cavalry and Japanese troops. The entourage was attacked at a narrow crossroads by two Japanese fanatics armed with long swords and the attackers caused considerable casualties before one was quickly killed and the other incapacitated. In a letter to his wife Parkes wrote:

> I saw some confusion among the last horses … immediately a Japanese rushed past us cutting frantically at everybody as he ran. His blows cleared me, but cut my belt and took off the nose of Satow's pony, which was close to me. I called out to our men to cut him down, and he was bayoneted before he got to the end of the guard, one of whom he severely wounded.[15]

A more graphic description was provided by Mitford in a letter to *The Times* of 20 May 1868. He also gave details of the part played by the Japanese members of the entourage, particularly Nakai Kōzō, 'a Japanese officer of rank, formerly of the Satsuma clan', and Gotō Kōjirō, 'a high officer of the Foreign Department'. Nakai tried to cut down the attackers but stumbled on his long trousers and was himself cut. Gotō came to his rescue and between the two of them they killed and decapitated one of the attackers. The other fanatic, despite having been cut, bayoneted, lanced and shot in the head, survived and on later interrogation was discovered to be a renegade priest with no motives other than to kill any foreigners he met. As events quietened down, Parkes had exclaimed to Mitford, 'Sensation diplomacy this, Mitford!', before returning to the British legation. The court expressed its deepest regret at the incident and Parkes left matters of retribution entirely in the hands of the new government, suggesting that any future attacks on foreigners by Japanese be punished by an ignoble death.[16]

Queen Victoria presented 'swords of honour to both Nakai and Gotō, in token of her appreciation of their gallantry on this occasion'. The Kyoto National Museum has in its collection the original faded documents from Parkes to Nakai thanking him for his (and Gotō's) efforts in defending the British party and one of the presentation swords in its original box. The sword is modelled on the English army officer's curved Mameluk pattern levée sword by Charles Smith and Co. of 5 New Burlington Street, London. Quite what the Japanese made of this, perhaps to their eyes, bizarre sword has not been recorded.

The Westerners were particularly impressed by the effectiveness of the swords of the samurai and there is a grudging respect paid towards them, and the stern resolve of the samurai, in the many accounts of the hard life to which diplomats had to endure in these early days in Japan. Seppuku was still regarded as a viable form of honourable execution, and the young British diplomat, Algernon Bertram Mitford, attended such an event as an official witness. The self-immolation was to be carried out by Taki Zensaburō who had ordered an attack on the foreign settlements in February 1868. Mitford described the event in his book *Tales of Old Japan*, the execution taking place at 10.30 at night at the temple of Seifukuji 'on the orders of the Mikado himself':

> Slowly, and with great dignity, the condemned man mounted on to the raised floor and prostrated himself before the high altar twice, and seated himself on the felt carpet with his back to the high altar, the kaishaku crouching on his left-hand side. One of the three attending officers then came forward bearing a stand on which, wrapped in paper, lay the *wakizashi*, the short sword or dirk of the Japanese, nine inches and a half in length, with a point and an edge as sharp as a razor's… Deliberately and with a steady hand he took the dirk that lay before him; he looked at it wistfully, almost affectionately; for a moment he seemed to collect his thoughts for the last time, and then stabbing himself deeply below the waist on the left-hand side, he drew the dirk slowly across to the right side and, turning it in the wound, gave a slight cut upwards. During this sickeningly painful operation, he never moved a muscle of his face. When he drew out the dirk, he leaned forward and stretched out his neck; an expression of pain for the first time crossed his face, but he uttered no sound. At that moment the *kaishaku* who, still crouching by his side, had been watching his every movement, sprang to his feet, poised his sword for a second in the air; there was a flash, a heavy, ugly thud, a crashing fall; with one blow the head had been severed from the body. A dead silence followed, broken only by the hideous noise of the blood throbbing out of the inert heap before us, which but a moment before had been a brave and chivalrous man. It was horrible.[17]

The dissolution of the samurai

There were attempts by some in the new Japanese parliament to adopt wholly Western ideals and in 1869 a proposal was made to ban seppuku. In a house of 209 members 200 voted against it, six abstained and only three approved the motion. During the debate seppuku was described as 'the very shrine of the Japanese national spirit and the embodiment in practice of devotion to principle'.[18] Nationalistic feeling was further expressed by one speaker who said: 'We ought to maintain a custom which fosters a sense of shame in the military caste and in the existence of which doubtless consists the supremacy of Japan over other countries.'[19] Another proposal around the same time to make the samurai tradition of the wearing of two swords optional rather than compulsory was unanimously voted down.

Mitford again quotes one of the speakers at that time whose speech mirrored the thoughts of the eighteenth-century exponents of bushidō.

> It is a good maxim for the soldier in peacetime never to forget war. What shall we say of a measure that asks us, even in the midst of civil disorder, to forget the existence of civil disorder? What, I ask is the character of the times in which we live? The object of the military caste wearing two swords is that they may suppress war by war; but as the chief glory of the sword consists in its resting in its sheath, it follows that a natural stimulus is given to letters.[20]

Many of those involved in the imperial restoration could not have foreseen that their

wish to recreate Japan in the model of an ideal past would result in the inevitable demise of the samurai. A great number of the emergent leaders in the new national government did in fact come from the privileged samurai class, but the more enlightened among them realized that there was no place in the modern world for the samurai as a distinct warrior class. The elite status of the samurai was also inconsistent with the demands for a national conscripted army, although most of the officer class were of samurai descent. The samurai as a class was officially abolished in a series of measures culminating in the Haitōrei Edict of March 1876 which finally ended the samurai privilege of carrying swords, weapons which had been central to their authority. These moves were seen by many of the samurai as far too radical and opposition was vociferous. Later the same year the voluntary option for the senior samurai to convert their hereditary stipends (traditionally evaluated in rice) into cash was made compulsory.

58 Woodblock print by Yoshitoshi, dated Meiji 10, 8th month (equivalent to 1877), from a series entitled *Kagoshima Seitō Zenki no Uchi* (Complete Account of the Chastisement at Kagoshima). With explosions in the background, troops ferociously fight to the death, armed with swords in traditional and Western-style mountings, as well as wearing traditional and Western-style uniforms. Note the tantō in the waist sashes of several of the combatants. These prints were produced immediately after the events mainly for the consumption of the residents of Tokyo who had a grudging respect for both sides in the Satsuma Rebellion. V&A: E.14197–1886.

The forbidden swords were on more than one occasion used to assassinate those government officials who had proposed and implemented these radical reforms.

There were still power struggles within the Meiji oligarchy, and some samurai leaders who had either been excluded from government positions or had taken offence at the disestablishment of the samurai class undertook armed rebellion. The great Satsuma Rebellion of 1877 was a test of the new government's conscript army, who were armed with modern weapons against the traditionally armed Satsuma samurai, pitting former samurai and conscripted farmers against those who maintained the traditions of 1,000 years. The rebels in extreme cases refused to use guns, preferring instead to fight with the traditional weapons of the samurai, the sword, spear, bow and naginata, thereby perpetuating some of the mystique of the samurai. Their philosophy was that it was better to die using traditional weapons than modern ones. Unsurprisingly, the rebels

59 Tachi blade with inscriptions 'Tomomitsu' and 'Kemmu ni nen' (equivalent to 1335) in the Northern Court of the Nambokuchō period. This graceful blade, with its long kissaki typical of the Nambokuchō period, has been considerably shortened and the inscriptions have been inlaid in gold. Any original inscriptions would have been lost during the shortening of the blade. The sword (see plate 60 for the mounting) was given by the Emperor Meiji to Sir Harry Parkes on the occasion of his private audience in May 1871. Parkes subsequently gave the sword to the South Kensington Museum (later the V&A).

V&A: M.13–1949, Parkes Bequest.

were defeated and their leader Saigō Takamori, who had been instrumental in the restoration of the emperor's power, took his own life (plate 58).

Saigō Takamori inspired his followers, and others, with his dedication to the spirit of bushidō. One of his noted sayings was: 'One who wants neither life, nor name, nor rank nor money is hardly to be controlled. It is only such indomitable men who can carry great affairs of state through adversity to completion.'[21] It is indicative of the Japanese respect for the samurai spirit that in later years Saigō Takamori was posthumously pardoned, had his full honour restored and emerged as a hero of modern Japanese nationalism and militarism; and his statue can be seen today in Ueno Park in Tokyo.

The swordsmiths and metalworkers under Emperor Meiji

With swords no longer playing an important role in everyday samurai wear, there were suddenly vast numbers of craftsmen, swordsmiths, metalworkers and specialist makers of the various sword fittings (as well as armourers and associated trades) without a regular source of income. Some used their skills to produce finely crafted everyday objects or, with the adoption of Western-style fashion, items of jewellery which had never previously been worn by the Japanese. Tobacco smoking became ever more popular and smoking sets with metal fittings were worn at the waist by fashionable people. Some swordsmiths had a source of income from making 'official' swords for dedication to shrines or temples or as fine hand-forged swords to be carried on official occasions or by senior officers in the new national army or navy (plates 59 and 60). These types of swords were increasingly mounted in Western military styles to go with the adopted Western-style uniforms, or on occasions as sword-sticks which could be carried in public places (although this was of dubious legality).

Some metalworkers continued to produce superb, although totally impractical, examples of sword fittings. These pieces were never meant to be mounted on swords but were *tour de force* examples of the craftsman's work, employing many variations of inlaid and patinated soft metals (plate 61). This was also the period when the Japanese government was promoting the work of their craftsmen through the flourishing world trade expositions of the latter half of the nineteenth century, and sword fittings featured at many of these events. With the sword and its accessories no longer required in Japan itself, huge numbers of weapons and fittings were exported to the West and it is from this time that fine collections of Japanese sword-related metalwork find their way into European collections. The range and styles of objects produced by the hundreds of schools of Japanese metalworkers appealed to the taste of late nineteenth-century Western collectors who were obsessed with the taxonomy of objects and this, linked to the craze for Japanese art at that time, was a heaven-sent opportunity to collect.

Notable among the metalworkers at this time was Kanō Natsuo (1828–98), a machi-bori craftsman from Kyoto who had been apprenticed to a swordsmith since the age of seven. In 1840 he began to study metalworking and by 1854 he had moved to Edo to continue his studies and eventually set up an independent workshop. His work was of such high quality that he was commissioned by the newly restored Emperor Meiji (who had a particular love of swords) to make a new mounting (along with some of his abler pupils) for the Suiryū Ken, the Nara-period chokutō held in the Shōsōin. Other metalworkers adopted the traditional techniques associated with sword fittings to produce

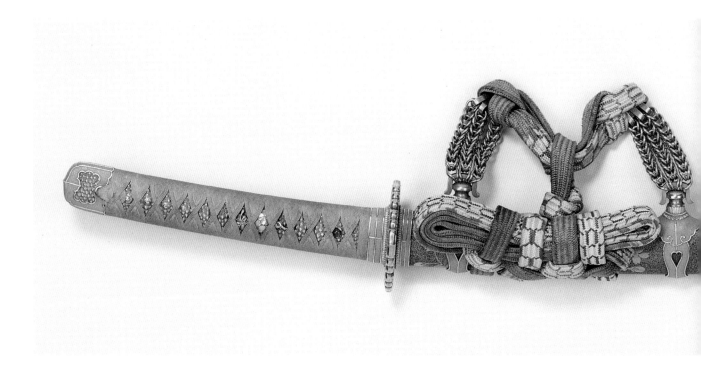

60 Ito-maki no tachi (see plate 59 for the blade) superbly mounted in a gold lacquered scabbard decorated with *hira-makie* blossoms on a *makie* background; even the *same* (ray skin) on the hilt is lacquered with gold. The metal fittings are of solid gold (including the suspension chains) by Ōta Yoshihisa. The fittings, as well as the mounting, appear to have been made especially for the presentation of the sword to Parkes, as a lengthy dedicatory inscription underneath the tsuba is dated to the second month of 1871. V&A: M.13–1949, Parkes Bequest.

excellent ornamental metal objects. For example, Komai Otojirō (1842–1917) of Kyoto used the technique of inlaying gold into iron tsuba (*hira zōgan*) to produce many richly decorated iron objects which have found their way into numerous private and public collections. It is indicative of the changes in Japanese taste that most of these pieces were for export, and at the time of writing the Tokyo National Museum is seeking to acquire its first piece by Komai (plate 62).

The latter half of the nineteenth century saw the rise of Japan as a world military power and with this rise came a renewed interest in the traditional sword. Foremost among the smiths at this time was Gassan Sadakazu (1836–1918). The Gassan tradition of sword making had originated in the mountains of Dewa province where it was known as Dewa Sanzan (the three mountains of Dewa) and was rooted in the ascetic Buddhist practices of Shugendō, whose adherents were the Shugensha, better known as the Yamabushi. Shugendō in Dewa was immensely influential in the region from the late Heian period, and the power of the sect was at its height during the Kamakura period. During these warring periods the swordsmiths worked exclusively for the Dewa Sanzan and rarely signed their blades, using the simple signature Gassan on rare occasions. It was not until 1470 that the first dated blade is to be found. The distinctive characteristics of the Gassan school is their *ayasugi-hada*, a concentrically wavy grain in the blade. Subsequent prohibitions against religious orders carrying swords saw the eventual disappearance of the Gassan school.

Gassan Sadayoshi (1800–1870) was born in Dewa province but moved to Edo around 1820 and entered the school of the swordsmith Suishinshi Masahide. He moved to Osaka around 1830 to set up his own school, having already gained quite a reputation for his work in Edo. His own son died in infancy so he adopted the son of Tsukamoto

61 Tsuba, *c.*1880. A Ni-ō (Buddhist deity) carrying a *vajra* (ritual thunderbolt) glares fiercely out of the tsuba while an impish *oni* (demon) peeks through the hole for a kozuka as if from behind a cloud. The tsuba is of russet-patinated iron with inlay of gold and high relief decoration of gold and silver, and the design fully exploits the potentials of this otherwise restrictive shape. The tsuba is signed on the reverse by Hata Nobuyoshi.
V&A: M.1209–1931, Hildburgh Gift.

62 Tachi mounting, *c*.1870–90, for a blade by Gassan Sadakazu (plate 63). The scabbard of wood is covered with iron sheet decorated with dragons, phoenix, shishi and *mon* (family crests) in silver and gold *hira-zōgan* (flat inlay). The scabbard is signed in a silver cartouche 'Nihon Koku Kyoto No Ju Komai Tsukuru' (made by Komai of Kyoto, Japan).

V&A: M.48–1971, Gift of the L.A. Mayer Memorial Foundation.

Shichirōbei who in time took the name Gassan Sadakazu. From the age of eleven Sadakazu began to learn the traditions of the Gassan school which Sadayoshi had revived. In addition to the characteristic ayasugi-hada, he made blades in the Bizen and Sōshū styles (plate 63). The 1876 prohibition against swords reduced his output considerably and he made a living mostly from producing copies of ancient blades. He seems to have resumed production around 1887 at a time when Japan was beginning her imperialistic expansions. In 1905 he was appointed to the distinguished position of 'Imperial Arts and Crafts Expert', a system initiated by the Emperor Meiji, who had a particular interest in the Japanese sword, to promote the best of Japan's traditional craftsmen (plate 64). Gassan Sadakazu's descendants continue his traditions today, and his grandson, Gassan Sadaichi (1907–95) carried the nationally designated title of 'Important Intangible Cultural Property', a position generally referred to as 'Living National Treasure'.

The sword in the modern period

The demand for fine swords for state occasions and for consecration at Shintō shrines such as the Great Shrine at Ise ensured that the traditions of the sword did not die out. The sword remained a symbol of authority throughout Japan's imperialist period when the conscript army was led, for the most part, by officers of samurai stock. Higher-ranking officers during the wars against China and Russia frequently carried well-made blades (mounted in Western styles) but NCOs would be issued with inferior quality blades (plate 65).

63 Katana blade signed
'Naniwa ju, Gassan Unryushi
Sadakazu hori do saku [+ seal
with character for 'Sada' inside]'
(Gassan Unryushi Sadakazu of
Naniwa [Osaka] made and
carved this) and 'Meiji ni hebi
doshi hachi gatsu hi' (second
year of Meiji, Snake year
[equivalent to 1869], a day in
the eighth month). The blade
has a splendid horimono of a
dragon chasing a flaming pearl
on the omote and a vajra-
handled ken and bonji
(perhaps of the Buddhist deity
Marishiten) on the ura
(see plate 62 for the mounting).
V&A: M.48–1971, Gift of the L.A. Mayer
Memorial Foundation.

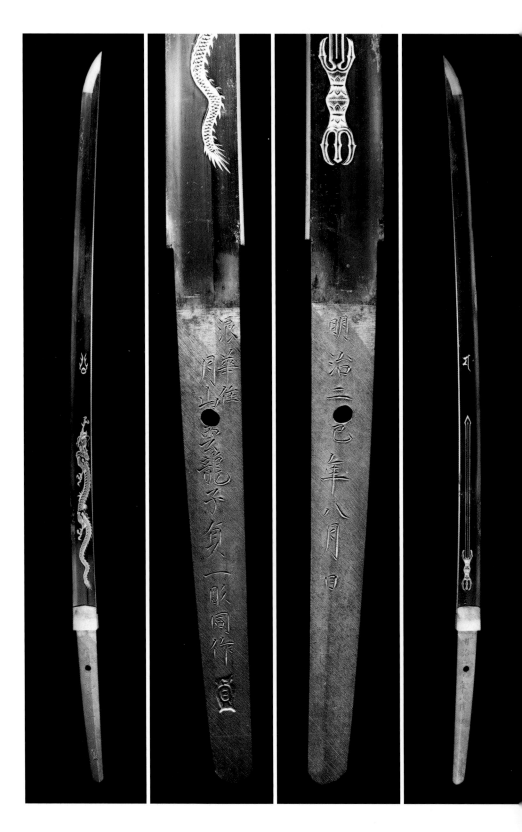

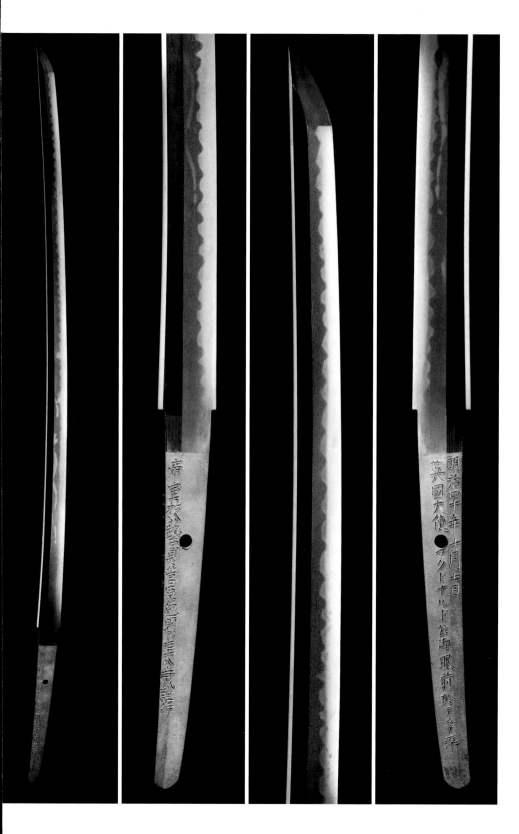

64 Tachi blade signed 'Teishitsu Gigei-in Sugawara Kanenori, Nana-ju hachi sai, Kin Saku' (Sugawara Kanenori, Craftsman of the Imperial Household, aged 78 years, respectfully made this) and 'Meiji Yon-ju nen, Ju gatsu, Shichi nichi, Eikoku Taishi Makudonarudo-ko Go-ganzen ni oite kore O niragu' (seventh day, tenth month of the fortieth year of the reign of Emperor Meiji [equivalent to 1907], respectfully tempered before the British Ambassador MacDonald). This elegant blade has a subtle tempering pattern of a stylized dragon near the shinogi of both sides of the blade.

V&A: M.136–1929, MacDonald Gift.

65 A scene from the Sino-Japanese War in a print entitled 'Taiwan-tō kiryū konoeshidan Funsen Tekigun o gekihe' (the Imperial Guard division based on Taiwan crushing the enemy army after a furious fight), by Toshihide and dated equivalent to 1895. The officers leading the charge are clearly carrying traditional swords mounted in Western style. Their conscript troops carry single-action bolt rifles and one also has a bayonet suspended from his belt. The Imperial Navy's Rising Sun flag (together with the 'Hinomaru' national flag) and a powerful battleship (probably one of those made in Newcastle, England) can also be seen in the background. These types of prints were produced immediately after the events they depicted and were effective instruments of propaganda in Japan's imperialistic expansion period. V&A: E.812–1945.

From the 1920s onwards during the Japanese expansion into Asia a new form of mounted sword emerged, the *shin-guntō*. Most of these were machine-made from a single piece of steel in arsenals, frequently in the town of Seki, which had previously mass-produced blades during the Muromachi period. The blades were rarely signed – sometimes, if hand-finished, they would bear a signature – but were generally simply stamped with the arsenal mark and number. It was rare for an officer to have a sword which was a family heirloom remounted to take into battle, as the possibility of such a blade being captured or destroyed could not be countenanced.

Together with Japan's imperialist expansion came what can be justly regarded as a total corruption of the traditional values of bushidō, and the excesses committed at that time in the name of the emperor and bushidō have unfortunately clouded the history of the Japanese sword. The absolute loyalty and devotion in service to one's lord which the samurai had traditionally observed was now to be dedicated to the emperor as the national figurehead, who was regarded as a divine being, descended directly from the Sun Goddess Amaterasu. Military service at that time was an obligation and to die for the emperor and one's country was a privilege.

Following defeat in 1945 the Japanese mainland was occupied by Allied forces and thousands of swords were surrendered, an act which perhaps the occupying forces did not fully comprehend at the time. Prior to this time the spirit of bushidō had been hijacked by nationalism, but the sword still remained the most potent symbol of the samurai ethos. To surrender the sword meant total submission. The majority of these swords were worthless pieces of machine-made metal, but many were finely crafted blades. Estimates of the number of swords surrendered at this time vary between 172,000 and as many as 3,000,000, all these from private individuals. The post-war occupying forces ordered the destruction of the sword as a weapon of war and as a potent

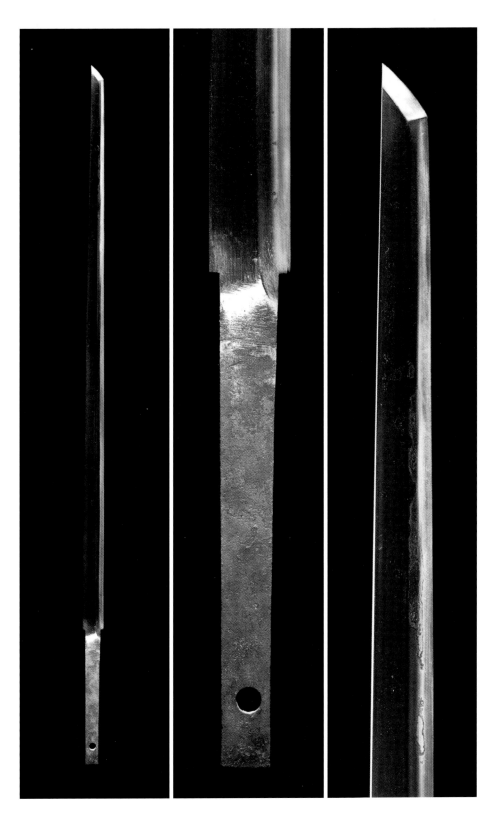

66 Copy of a Chokutō. This sword was originally believed to be an imitation of the Suiryū Ken (plate 1), but it is substantially different from that blade and was probably made in the late 19th century. It does, however, have its own interesting history. Following the Allied occupation of Japan in 1945, all swords were banned and thousands confiscated. According to V&A documentation, a British Army officer on a visit to an American ordnance depot saw a pile of surrendered swords destined for the Mitsubishi Company where they were to be melted down and made into cutlery. He was permitted to take as many as he wanted and he enlisted the help of Inami Hakusui to have his selection polished and mounted in shirasaya in Tokyo. On his return to the UK with his swords, the V&A purchased just this one example from the dozens he had selected.

V&A: M.60–1954.

symbol which epitomized Japan's militaristic recent past. The order in November 1945 stipulated that 'all swords, including privately owned swords, shall be treated as symbols of militarism and destroyed'. The manufacture of swords at this time was also banned. Many of these surrendered swords were 'liberated' as souvenirs by Allied troops and taken back to their homes (plate 66).

This order was applied strictly to the modern shin-guntō but was subsequently modified to exclude swords belonging to museums, temples, shrines and those in private collections which were deemed to be of artistic merit. The question of what defined an 'art sword' was a thorny one and in 1946 thousands of swords were taken to the Tokyo Imperial Household Museum and then to the army's Akabane supply depot, where between May and December 1947 they were assessed. Over 5,000 were deemed to fit the category of 'art sword' and these were taken to the newly designated National Museum (successor to the Imperial Museum) to be returned to their owners. This definition of 'art sword' had thereby allowed many swords to escape destruction by the occupying forces. From this time on any swords still held in private hands had to be registered with the local police. It is also interesting to note that the first special exhibition to be held at the new National Museum (on 25 May 1947) was entitled 'An Exhibition of the Art of the Sword'.

Despite the post-war ban, in 1949 permission was granted for the production of sixty swords as part of the cyclical twenty-year renewal ceremony at the Great Shrine at Ise. In 1953 a new law was passed which allowed the production of swords with the permission of the Committee for the Protection of Cultural Properties, and the following year the Society for the Preservation of Japanese Art Swords (Nihon Bijutsu Tōken Hozon Kyōkai, or NBTHK), which had been founded in 1948 to administer the 'Akabane' swords, held its first exhibition of contemporary blades. This society is extremely active today, stating in its articles that 'this association is dedicated to the preservation and public display of swords valued as works of art or craft...' and equally striving to promote the modern sword, gendaitō, to ensure that it is of the highest quality expected of the nihontō, the 'Japanese art sword'.

67 Open-air sword fencing at the Fukugawa Hachiman Temple in Tokyo. An annual summer festival dedicated to the warlike deity Hachiman takes place in Tokyo centred on this temple. There are open-air displays of kendō in the temple precincts as well as demonstrations of the use of real swords. The two combatants in this photograph exercise superb skill in the control of their swords, stopping only just short of delivering the final cut.

Photograph by Gregory Irvine.

Today the Japanese sword, despite nearly disappearing under post-war prohibitions, is regarded as an art object in itself, although some people disapprove of its original function and of the links with the nationalistic movements of the early twentieth century. The martial art of swordsmanship still flourishes with schools of kendō, the way of the sword, and iai-dō, another form of swordsmanship, active throughout the world (plate 67). The state system of preserving traditional crafts through the designation of 'Important Intangible Cultural Properties' has allocated this title to two contemporary swordsmiths, Amata Akitsugu and Ōsumi Toshihira. It is both an honour and obligation to bear this title and the holders have a duty to ensure that the skills behind their particular crafts are perpetuated. Many smiths today are expressing themselves in new ways, although some are criticised for their apparent overuse of excessively flamboyant hamon and for catering overmuch to the tastes of their contemporary patrons. In this, however, they are little different from their historical forebears.

Within Japan there are research institutes such as that which attempts to restore those traditional sword-manufacturing techniques of the Bizen schools which are necessary to reproduce the unique characteristics of that particular style. Osafune in modern-day Okayama prefecture, the old province of Bizen, is still a thriving centre for sword production. Throughout Japan there are dedicated collectors and connoisseurs of both the traditional and the contemporary sword who dedicate their lives to the promotion and understanding of the Japanese sword as a unique art form. The demand for the Japanese sword, particularly in the perhaps less discerning Western world, is such that it is even possible to buy 'hand-forged swords', of possibly questionable quality, via the Internet. In recent years glossy magazines have also offered for sale 'traditional Japanese swords' manufactured by the 'fabled swordsmiths of Toledo, Spain'! However, in many other countries around the world there are serious and dedicated societies and individual collectors whose aim is to promote a better understanding and appreciation of the Japanese art sword.

What of the samurai today? Both the samurai and his ideals are now far removed from the original, and he is seen as a romantic hero, popularized in the Japanese equivalent of the Western and appearing in costume dramas, particularly of the Sengoku Jidai, and in genre films. There are numerous samurai-themed *manga*, comics aimed at children and adults alike, which glorify the attributes of the samurai (plate 68). He serves as a symbol of strength and reliability in the world of advertising and can be used to sell anything from cars to soft drinks. In the West, too, the samurai has been a model for the idealized warrior. The films of the Japanese director Akira Kurosawa have gone some considerable way to maintaining this ideal and have inspired many Western directors. Kurosawa's *The Seven Samurai* inspired

68 Illustration from the story 'Muyōnosuke' in the manga *Ran*, special edition vol. 4, no. 14, written and illustrated by Saitō Takao, Tokyo 1999. The contemporary Japanese view of the samurai warrior is depicted in this comic book where the well-honed skills of the scarred hero overcome innumerable foes in the protection of the defenceless. Copyright Saitō Production Co., Ltd.

The Magnificent Seven, and *The Hidden Fortress* is said to have influenced much of the *Star Wars* series.

This last series of films contains themes which could just as easily have been written about attitudes prevalent in medieval Japan: honour, virtue, loyalty and the continuing fight against oppression. The costume worn by the evil Darth Vader is not dissimilar to samurai armour, especially the black plate armour of Date Masamune. The similarities in fighting techniques are particularly evident in the use of the 'light sabre', a weapon on which the Jedi knight totally relies and in which lies his honour. It is wielded in the same two-handed fashion as the Japanese sword. The attitude towards the introduction of the gun into Japan and the reverence given to the sword is also reflected in the words of the Jedi master Obi-Wan Kenobi when he gives Luke Skywalker, the young potential Jedi knight, his father's light sabre with the words: 'It is not as clumsy or as random as a blaster, it is an elegant weapon for a more civilized age; use it well Luke.'[22]

Our perception of the ideals of the samurai is emphasised even further by the use of the term 'samurai' when adopted by Westerners. One of the most recent examples of this which I have come across concerns 'samurai' as applied to a dedicated group of computer hackers. To quote from the on-line 'Jargon Dictionary', a 'samurai' is:

> A hacker who hires out for legal cracking jobs, snooping for factions in corporate political fights, lawyers pursuing privacy-rights and First Amendment cases, and other parties with legitimate reasons to need an electronic locksmith. In 1991, main-stream media reported the existence of a loose-knit culture of samurai ... mostly bright teenagers with personal micros; they have modelled themselves explicitly on the historical samurai of Japan... Those interviewed claim to adhere to a rigid ethic of loyalty to their employers and to disdain the vandalism and theft practiced by criminal crackers as beneath them and contrary to the hacker ethic; some quote Miyamoto Musashi's *Book of Five Rings*, a classic of historical samurai doctrine, in support of these principles.[23]

Despite the excesses committed with the sword during Japan's imperialistic advances of the early twentieth century when blind obedience and mindless unquestioning loyalty to the emperor prevailed, the legacy of bushidō and the sword still has a strong influence in modern Japan. Today, the loyalty previously dedicated to one's lord is now given to the company or to the school or university. The rigid self-discipline of the samurai is still evident in a Japanese society which expects that expressions of personal grief, resentment or joy are not for public display. It is telling that the introduction to the catalogue of the Tokyo National Museum's 1997 exhibition *The Japanese Sword: Iron Craftsmanship and the Warrior Spirit* states: 'Through the sword, which the Japanese people have come to treasure, we hope that you will appreciate both history and the warrior spirit which is the pride of the Japanese people.'

The philosophy behind the samurai ethic is perhaps best summed up by the words of the Japanese neo-Confucian scholar, Hayashi Razan (1583–1657), also called Dōshun, who lived through the end of the Momoyama period and into the Tokugawa period:

> To have the arts of peace, but not the arts of war is to lack courage. To have the arts of war, but not the arts of peace is to lack wisdom. A man who is dedicated and has a mission is called a samurai. A man who is of inner worth and upright conduct, who has moral principles and mastery of the arts, he is also called a samurai.[24]

Notes

1. Joly, *Swords and Samé*, p.2.

2. Blomberg, *The Heart of the Warrior*, p.110 (quoting from 'The Tale of the Heike' and 'Hōgen Monogatari', trans. Kitagawa Hiroshi and Bruce Tsuchida, *Transactions of the Asiatic Society of Japan*, vol. XLV, part I, Tokyo 1917).

3. Speake, *Cultural Atlas of Japan*, p.126.

4. Hakusui, *Nippontō, The Japanese Sword*, pp.147–8.

5. Satō, *The Japanese Sword*, p.88.

6. Blomberg, *The Heart of the Warrior*, p.57 (quoting Michael S.J. Cooper, *This Island of Japon: João Rodrigues' Account of 16th Century Japan*, Tokyo 1973).

7. Musashi, *A Book of Five Rings*, p.95.

8. Ibid., p.38.

9. Blomberg, *The Heart of the Warrior*, pp.69–70 (quoting Trevor Legget, *Zen and the Ways*, London 1978, pp.158–160).

10. Ibid., pp.160–62 (quoting W.T. de Bary, *Sources of Japanese Tradition*, New York 1964, pp.390–91).

11. Ibid., p.182 (quoting *Told Round a Brushwood Fire: The Autobiography of Arai Hakuseki*, trans. Joyce Ackroyd, Tokyo 1979, p.39).

12. Ibid. (quoting *Lessons from History, the Dokushi Yoron by Arai Hakuseki*, trans. Joyce Ackroyd, University of Queensland Press, 1982, pp.236–7).

13. Sansom, *A History of Japan, 1615–1867*, pp.175–6.

14. Ibid.

15. Gregory Irvine, '"Sensation Diplomacy!" Sir Harry Parkes and Japan, 1865–1871', *Royal Armouries Yearbook*, vol.2, 1997, p.157.

16. Ibid.

17. A.B. Mitford, *Tales of Old Japan*, London 1890, pp.355–60.

18. Cortazzi, *Mitford's Japan*, pp.159–160.

19. Ibid.

20. Ibid.

21. Trevor Leggett, *The Tiger's Cave: Translations of Japanese Zen Texts*, London 1977, p.173.

22. George Lucas (writer and director), soundtrack of *Star Wars*, 1977.

23. 'The Jargon Dictionary': http://www.netmeg.net/jargon/.

24. W.T. de Bary (ed.), *Sources of Japanese Tradition*, New York 1958, vol.I, p.347.

Glossary

aiguchi: mounted sword or dagger having no tsuba

ashi: lines of martensitic steel from the hamon to the edge of the blade

ayasugi-hada: concentric and wavy graining of the ji, said to resemble the grain of the cryptomeria tree

bōshi: the hamon within the kissaki

chikei: bright lines of nie in the ji

chōji hamon: hamon with irregular shapes said to resemble the buds of the clove flower

chokutō: straight, single-edged sword of the Kofun and Nara periods

daishō: matching pair of swords consisting of the katana and wakizashi

fuchi: ring-shaped oval metal fitting on the hilt of a sword next to the tsuba, often decorated to match the kashira

fumbari: characteristic typically found in blades of the Heian period where the width of the sword increases suddenly at the base of the blade adjacent to the hilt

gunome: hamon of regular, sharply undulating curves

ha: the tempered edge of the blade

hada: surface steel of the blade used to describe the grain structure (see also ji)

hamachi: notch in the edge of the blade which defines the start of the nakago

hamon: crystalline temper-line formed near the cutting edge of a blade marking the transition between martensitic and pearlite steels

hi: a groove carved into the blade

hira ji: the angled ground of the blade between the ha and the shinogi

hira-zukuri: triangular sectioned flat-sided blade (with no shinogi)

hitatsura: tempering marks visible over much of the surface of the blade

horimono: decorative or religious carving in the blade

ito-maki no tachi: style of tachi mounting, developed in the late Momoyama period, where the scabbard between and either side of the suspension straps is wrapped with braid in order to prevent the lacquer on the scabbard from abrading against armour

inazuma: lines of nie within and around the hamon

iriyamagata-jiri: butt-end of the nakago with an asymmetrical 'V' shape

itame: wood-grain ji resembling a board cut against the grain

ji: the 'ground' of the blade (see also hada)

kaiken: a short dagger, generally carried by women

kantō tachi: straight, single-edged sword with an annular pommel, Yayoi and Kofun periods

kashira: pommel on the hilt of the sword, usually of metal and frequently decorated to form a matching pair with the fuchi

katakiri-ha zukuri: style of sword blade with one side completely flat, the other having a shinogi

katana: sword worn with the cutting edge uppermost

kazari-dachi: decorative mounted tachi used at court since the Nara period

ken: a double-edged straight sword associated with Buddhist ritual

kinsuji: lines of nie within the hamon, similar to, but shorter than, inazuma

kissaki: the pointed area of the blade

kissaki moroha zukuri: single-edged blade with a shinogi but double-edged near the point

ko-itame: fine itame graining

kōgai: small bodkin-like implement carried in a pocket in the scabbard *kogatana*: small knife carried in a pocket in the scabbard

ko-nie: extremely fine, yet visible grains of nie in the blade

kojiri: chape of the scabbard, of varying forms but usually metal and sometimes with decoration which matches the kashira

koshigatana: 'waist sword', an early term for a type of short sword typically with no tsuba

koshi-zori: curvature near or in the nakago of the blade

kotō: 'old' swords, i.e. made before 1596

kozuka: the hilt of the kogatana (sometimes this term is erroneously used for the kogatana)

kuri-jiri: butt-end of the nakago with a rounded asymmetrical 'V' shape

kurikata: 'chestnut shape' on the side of the scabbard of a wakizashi or katana, through which passes the cord used to secure the scabbard to a sash

masame: fine graining of the ji with lines running parallel to the shinogi

mei: smith's signature on the nakago

mekugi-ana: hole in the nakago for the retaining peg which passes through the hilt

menuki: decorative metal fitting under the bindings of both sides of the hilt which serves additionally to provide a better grip on the sword

midareba: irregular hamon

mitsugashira: the point at which the shinogi and yokote meet

mokume: burl-wood graining of the ji

mon: family crest used as a decorative motif on armour, metal sword fittings and on lacquered scabbards

mune: the back of the blade

munemachi: notch in the back of the blade which defines the beginning of the nakago

nagasa: length of the blade, being defined as the distance between the munemachi and the point of the kissaki

naginata: polearm with a long, curved, sword-like blade

nakago: the unpolished hilt of the blade (the tang)

nakagojiri: the butt-end of the nakago

nie: visible grains of martensitic steel in a blade, described as having the appearance of frost on grass

nioi: minute particles of martensitic steel in a blade which form misty patterns

notareba: gently undulating hamon

omote: the side of the nakago (usually bearing the signature) which faces away from the body when the sword is worn

saki-zori: blade with the centre of its curvature nearer to the tip

sambonsugi: hamon with sharp undulations in groups of three, said to resemble tops of the cryptomeria tree

shakudō: alloy of copper (approximately 95%) and gold (approximately 5%) which is generally patinated to a rich black colour

shibuichi: alloy of copper (approximately 75%) and silver (approximately 25%) which is patinated to give a wide variety of colours from silver to brown as well as a range of greys

shinogi: longitudinal ridge which separates the back of the sword from the angled cutting edge

shinogi ji: the ground of the blade between the shinogi and the mune

shin-shintō: revivalist swords made from around 1800 which copied cut-down kotō

shintō: swords made after 1596 but before approximately 1800

shirasaya: plain wooden scabbard (traditionally magnolia wood), in which a blade is kept when not mounted for wear

sori: curvature of the blade, being defined as the greatest distance between the imaginary line of the nagasa and the mune

sudareba: hamon formed of several lines (resembling the horizontal strips of a bamboo screen)

suguha: straight hamon

sunagashi: thick lines of nie which follow the line of the hamon

suriage: term used to describe swords cut down at the nakago

tachi: sword worn with the cutting edge downwards

tantō: literally a short sword, but generally applied to a longer form of dagger

tōranha: hamon of large irregular outline

torii-zori: curvature in the middle of the blade

tsuba: sword guard

uchi-zori: blade with a slight curvature towards the cutting edge

ura: the side of the nakago which faces in towards the body when the sword is worn

utsuri: a shadow-like crystalline structure in the ji which appears to reflect the hamon

wakizashi: short companion sword (worn with the katana)

ya-no-ne: general term for an arrow-head

yari: general term for a spear which can be of varying length and configuration

yasurime: file marks on the nakago

yō: detached ashi-like areas of martensitic steel within the hamon

yokote: a small ridge-line at right angles to the shinogi which defines the area of the kissaki

yoroi-doshi: a thick, armour-piercing hira-zukuri dagger

zukuri: 'form' of the blade, i.e. shinogi-zukuri: a blade having a shinogi (see also hira-zukuri)

Bibliography

Blomberg, Catharina. *The Heart of the Warrior: Origins and Religious Background of the Samurai System in Feudal Japan* (Folkestone 1994)

Compton, W.A.. *Nippon-to, Art Swords of Japan* (New York 1976): contributions by Junji Homma, Kanzan Sato and Morihiro Ogawa

Cortazzi, Hugh, ed. *Mitford's Japan: The Memoirs and Recollections, 1866–1906, of Algernon Bertram Mitford, the first Lord Redesdale* (London 1985)

Friday, Karl F. *Hired Swords: The Rise of Private Warrior Power in Early Japan* (Stanford 1992)

Fujishiro, Matsuo. *Nihon Kotō Jiten* and *Nihon Shintō Jiten* (Tokyo 1975)

Hakusui, Inami. *Nippontō, The Japanese Sword* (Tokyo 1948)

Harris, Victor. 'Japanese Swords and the Bizen Tradition', *Arts of Asia* (May/June 1986), pp. 125–9

Harris, Victor and Ogasawara, Nobuo. *Swords of the Samurai*, exh. cat. (London 1990)

Hawley, William. *Japanese Swordsmiths* (Hollywood 1966)

Iimura, Yoshiaki. *Shin-Shintō Taikan* (Tokyo 1966)

Ishii, Masakuni, ed. *Nippon Tō Meikan* (Tokyo 1976)

Joly, Henri L. and Inada, Hogitaro, *Swords and Samé* (London 1913): translations of Arai Hakuseki, *Sword Book in Honchō Gunkiko*, and Inaba Tsūriō, *Book of Samé*

Knutsen, R.M. *Japanese Polearms* (London 1963): includes section on arrows, based mainly on the V&A collections

Kokan, Nagayama. *The Connoisseur's Book of Japanese Swords*, trans. Mishina Kenji (Tokyo, London and New York 1997)

Musashi, Miyamoto. *A Book of Five Rings*, trans. Victor Harris (London 1974)

Ogasawara, Nobuo. *Nihontō no Kansho Kiso Chishiki* (Tokyo 1989, reprinted 1994)

Ogawa, Morihiro. *Japanese Master Swordsmiths: The Gassan Tradition*, exh. cat. (Museum of Fine Arts, Boston, 1989)

Robinson, B.W. *The Arts of the Japanese Sword* (London 1961, reprinted 1970)

Sansom, Sir George. *A History of Japan to 1334* (Stanford 1958); *A History of Japan, 1334–1615* (Stanford 1961); *A History of Japan, 1615–1867* (Stanford 1963)

Satō, Kanzan. *The Japanese Sword, a Comprehensive Guide*, trans. Joe Earle (Tokyo 1983)

Speake, Graham (ed), *Cultural Atlas of Japan* (Oxford 1988)

Stone, George Cameron. *A Glossary of the Construction, Decoration and Use of Arms and Armour in all Countries and in All Times (Together with Some Closely Related Subjects)* (New York 1961)

Tokugawa Art Museum. *Treasures from the Tokugawa Art Museum, vol. 3: Swords and Sword Fittings* (Nagoya 1998)

Tokyo National Museum. *The Japanese Sword: Iron Craftsmanship and the Warrior Spirit*, exh. cat. (Tokyo 1997)

Turnbull, Stephen. *The Samurai, a Military History* (London 1977)

Varley, Paul H. *Warriors of Japan as Portrayed in the War Tales* (Honolulu 1994)

Yoshihara, Yoshindo and Kapp, Leon and Hiroko. *The Craft of the Japanese Sword* (Tokyo 1987)

Web Pages

At the time of writing, the URLs below are correct and the pages have provided good, sound information. But, as with much Web-based information, the URLs may be subject to change. A word search on 'Japanese Swords' on the Web will produce thousands of addresses, but many of these pages should be treated cautiously, as there is at present much mis-information or poorly researched material on the Web.

'The Japanese Sword':
http://www.gemlink.com/~rstein/nihonto.htm

'Alan Quinn's Nihontō: the Japanese Sword':
http://www.meiboku.demon.co.uk/

'Tōken Society of Great Britain':
http://www.to-ken.com/

Index